OMAGH
Voices of Loss

OMAGH
Voices of Loss

GRAHAM SPENCER

Appletree Press

First published in 2005
by Appletree Press Ltd
The Old Potato Station
14 Howard Street South
Belfast
BT7 1AP

Tel: +44 (0) 28 90 24 30 74
Fax: +44 (0) 28 90 24 67 56
Web Site: www.appletree.ie
E-mail: reception@appletree.ie

Omagh – Voices of Loss

A catalogue record for this book
is available from the British Library.

ISBN 0 86281 978 4

Desk & Marketing Editor: Jean Brown
Editor: Jim Black
Design: Stuart Wilkinson
Production: Paul McAvoy

9 8 7 6 5 4 3 2 1

AP3291

Printed and Bound by J. H. Haynes & Co. Ltd.,
Sparkford

Contents

For those who speak in this book

Acknowledgements

Five years after the Omagh bomb of 1998 I wrote to all the families of those who died asking if they would like to talk to me about their experiences of that dreadful time and since. This book is the result of that initial enquiry. Despite my reservations that such a project would happen, I found that many decided they would like to speak with me. Some time after, I made arrangements to interview the families, going to Omagh and Buncrana for the bulk of the interviews, before then carrying out the remaining two in Guildford and Exeter. For me, the interviews were incredibly moving as well as shocking and they detail how lives are misshapen and damaged by terrorist violence. Moreover, as this material makes clear, this impact often resonates into the lives of victims much further than one might imagine, amplifying the experiences of suffering beyond the immediate and perhaps more obvious expectations of loss to a wider series of problems and pressures.

I could not have brought this material to print without the courage of Appletree Press and Jean Brown who have been supportive throughout. I would also like to thank Caroline Denyer for help with transcribing the interviews and my family and friends for their encouragement. It goes without saying that my particular thanks goes to Michael Gallagher without whose help this book would not exist. Lastly, although this material is dedicated to those affected by Omagh it is foremost a testimony to those brave and thoroughly decent people who are interviewed within these pages. To those people I am grateful in ways I cannot explain.

Foreword

Almost two years ago I was approached by Graham Spencer who asked if I would be interested in sharing my experiences of how my family coped with the death of our only son Aiden, one of thirty-one people who died in the Omagh bomb. I helped Graham as best I could, just as I have with the many others who have shown interest in Omagh over the years, but at that time I could not have imagined how successful Graham would be in his efforts of talking to those who lost loved ones in the bomb.

The Omagh bomb was the worst single act of terrorism in the history of Northern Ireland. But this book is not just about scale and statistics. It is about the human stories of many of the victims and their families. For me, the most difficult thing is trying to get people to look beyond the numbers and remember the individuals who died. In this book, stories of those individuals and what happened to them are told by the families, many of who talk for the first time in public. The least we can do is to read and learn about them.

It has been a difficult and at times dangerous road to travel these past seven years for all the victims of Omagh and from my experience that time has been filled with passion and pain along with considerable frustrations. Omagh has been described as the worst atrocity of the 'Troubles' but in reality, it occurred during what was supposed to be peacetime. So many had worked hard to secure that peace with The Good Friday Agreement of 1998 and that is why Omagh was shocking to so many. How could someone have carried out such a wicked and evil act? I for one was shocked when the so-called Real IRA proudly claimed responsibility, but was even more shocked to later discover that the Irish Government were in secret talks with the RIRA trying to broker a deal.

This was a bomb that killed mainly women and children. The bomb was deliberately parked outside the shop that sold school uniforms on the Saturday before the end of the school holidays and misleading warnings were given to maximise confusion. Everyone could identify with those affected from the unborn twins to grandmothers. This will probably be the largest number of victims of this atrocity to share their story with one writer and this is what makes this book so important. The stories here reflect the experiences of those who are the best placed to tell the world about the kind of people that died at Omagh along with their hopes, dreams and memories. To have secured interviews with fifteen of the families also says something about Graham's ability to gain the trust of so many.

Omagh was a very public atrocity and so the grieving progress was very much in the media. There has been much written and broadcast, including a full length feature film which highlights many of the difficulties the families faced in the early years. Sadly though, many of those issues remain unresolved. Many of the families feel that there can be no start to closure without justice and this can make everyday life stressful and for some meaningless. In the world we live in, mass murder by terrorism is becoming more commonplace and often takes place on a horrific scale. Less than three years after Omagh there was 9/11 where we witnessed thousands die on television. Along with this outrage we had the African Embassy attacks, the Bali bombing, the carnage at Madrid, the brutal murder of those in London and the ongoing horror of Iraq. All of us who have suffered through terrorism always feel the pain when we hear about a bombing where people have been murdered and mutilated. But, it is also important to not allow terrorism to stop us from doing what we want to do and to make sure that the human spirit overcomes the adversity which terrorism creates. Sometimes we need to reach deep inside ourselves for the strength to carry on and those in this book demonstrate that strength. Their voices reveal the spirit of human decency and the respect for life which terrorism tries to deny us. Whatever our thoughts, let us never forget the thirty-one men, women and children from Omagh, Buncrana and Madrid who died in the Omagh bombing on 15th August 1998.

Michael Gallagher

Introduction

The Good Friday Agreement signed on 10th April 1998 signalled the potential for a real and substantive peace in Northern Ireland. The television images which accompanied the exhaustive negotiations that culminated in the GFA indicated the possibility of hope and symbolised an end to the violence which had shaped Northern Ireland's history. It would not be an exaggeration to say that for many, 10th April 1998 heralded a new era of hope, opportunity and peace. The television images some four months later conveyed a very different reality however. Many will remember the amateur video footage with the date 15/8/98 visible in the corner of the screen which appeared across all the news networks. That footage showed audiences the immediate aftermath of a huge car bomb planted in Omagh by the Real IRA which ended the lives of twenty-nine people and unborn twins.

Within just a few months, the optimism of peace which surrounded the GFA had been ruthlessly shattered by the callous reality of terrorist violence. Here, through the lens of the amateur video camera could be seen the smog of debris, the blood, the torn clothes, the flapping arms of people in shock, the strewn possessions, the broken water mains, the noise of fire alarms randomly punctuated by the muffled cries of pain, and the erratic movements of people engulfed by trauma and disbelief. Through the dust and the mess, figures could be seen standing, bending, carrying, running, tending the injured and covering the dead. Within this chaos the images made it clear to all watching that the consequences of violence are always undeniably personal. It is people who absorb the effects of violence and it is people who carry the pain of suffering which that violence has imposed on them. Political and ideological arguments about the basis of violence often try, but can never escape this burden. As the amateur video footage made clear, terrorism murders people and crumples those who love the ones murdered. The impact is accumulative and inescapable no matter how those responsible try to evade that fact and present it as somebody else's fault. The images of Omagh with power and immediacy showed to all watching that no explanation for the violence could withstand the emotive reality of the death and misery which that violence had created.

Unfortunately, it is the motivation of terrorism and those who perpetuate it which has more often sustained the interests of writers, commentators and journalists when writing about violence. The lives of victims and how they exist with the weight of loss tend to receive far less attention than the broader and more dramatic narratives of terrorist organisations who reconstruct myths and imagined histories in order to continue doing what they do.

Personal stories of loss provide us with a narrative which is not constrained by such imaginations, however. Here, the small details of everyday existence and the emotive impact of suffering can be released from ideological conviction which all too often limits and obstructs expression of personal feeling and experience. But perhaps part of the appeal for those who try to write and talk about those engaged in violence lay in trying to find out why those who murder and injure people took that choice. In the case of victims, there is no choice. Those in Omagh on 15th August 1998 were given no choice about what happened. The victim's position in relation to the terrorist is one of complete powerlessness precisely because he or she does not and cannot know about what is going to happen, whereas the terrorist does. The terrorist has the choice to not act, but the victim cannot avoid the violence he or she is being subject to: there is no alternative but to bear its impact.

To begin with, the horror and emotiveness of the terrorist act attracts media interest and the rhetoric of politicians who make predictable announcements about perpetrators and responses. Those interviewed in this book all talk of the massive public response to their loss and the intense mass consumption of their grief in the days immediately after the bomb, which resulted in thousands of people visiting homes to show respect. But the intensity of this public concern fades almost as quickly as it starts and it is at that point, when the glare of the cameras moves away and the thousands who visited homes have gone, that the process of loss becomes the intimate, personal and lonely affair which it inevitably is. This book allows fifteen of those who lost loved ones in the bomb to articulate their experiences throughout the days after the bomb and since. The stories make for very emotional reading. They detail a range of similar and different reactions which all too clearly demonstrate the overwhelming sense of loss, the emptiness it creates and the strength needed to face it.

It is important to bear in mind though that there are a number of problems with a study of this kind. This is not the definitive story of those who suffered in Omagh. Hundreds were injured (many seriously) and there are those who lost loved ones who declined to be interviewed. They will have their own stories and experiences which although not here, are integral to understanding the impact of Omagh. We must also remember and respect those who find the prospect of talking about loss too painful to revisit. But accounting for these omissions, the interviews here refer to nearly half of those families who had loved ones murdered, making it a substantive testimony about suffering and loss and surviving the presence of both. There are difficulties with talking about suffering in relation to one atrocity. For those interviewed, being associated with Omagh has meant being associated with 'the single worst atrocity' in Northern Ireland, and this has brought exceptional levels of scrutiny and comment compared to the majority of atrocities committed in Northern Ireland, which have been individual and sometimes lacking in national (let alone international) attention. We must recognise that loss in all these cases is equally potent and omnipresent in the lives of those who must bear it. One need only look at the book *Lost Lives* (McKittrick *et al*) to sense that the 'Troubles' has created a social context which has destroyed lives with equal force regardless of religious or political persuasion. Unlike the process of violence which is discriminatory, the process of loss is non-discriminatory: who can say that any one person's loss is greater or lesser than anyone else's if the result is the same – devastated lives.

The testimonies of those in this book are direct, open and candid. Each interview begins with a short introductory statement about the person interviewed and the loved one(s) lost, before experiences and memories are conveyed verbatim. Many talk about losing children and having to identify their children in circumstances of almost unimaginable trauma. As one would expect, many of the interviews reveal similar actions and procedures which families had to follow in the immediate aftermath of the bomb: the unbearable waiting, hopes raised, hopes dashed, more unbearable waiting and then the news. The individual and collective experience of suffering during those formative stages after the bomb provide the stories with a cumulative power which is both moving and shocking. Memories and recollections of those early hours and days are then followed by the efforts made to rebuild lives in the months and years since. None of the interviews romanticise suffering. Rather they demonstrate how dealing with loss means carrying the endless imaginations of the future and the past, but not the present. The respondents refer to who their loved ones *were* and what they *could have been*, but can never refer to them as they *are*. It is continuing to live without access to the present in this way that creates the inescapable absence and suffering that victims of terrorism are forced to live with.

I can only thank those in this book for talking to me freely and honestly. When I asked them why they had decided to be interviewed, many responded that they made the decision in the hope that it might deter others from being involved in terrorism and committing murder. That if others could read about what terrorism does to people, they may turn away from its ruinous effects. Those in this book share experiences which they do not want others to have, but which they want others to know about. These are stories not from the 'safe' vantage point of political ideology but from the exposed vantage point of personal loss. In many ways, it seems objectionable to talk of such people as victims, because their stories reveal a strength of character and spirit which is not synonymous with being powerless. But we must bear in mind that these stories were not of individual making but have been imposed. It is that imposition which renders each testimony all the more remarkable, and which brings to light that only by resisting as well as accepting loss can one continue to live.

McKittrick, D. & Kelters, S. & Feeney, B. & Thornton, B. (1999) *Lost Lives*, Edinburgh: Mainstream.

Bernie Doherty

Bernie Doherty is interviewed at her home in Buncrana. She lost her eight-year-old son Oran in the bomb. Oran was on a student trip from Buncrana to Omagh which took place as part of an exchange with Spanish students. Oran died with two other children from Buncrana, James Barker and Sean McLaughlin (whose parents are also interviewed in this book), along with the Spanish schoolboy Fernando Blasco Baselga (12), and one of the Spanish organisers, Racio Abad Ramos (23).

He was eight years old and full of life, full of fun. Just a great wee boy, a funny wee boy, a real character. He loved football, going fishing and he was full of life. On the Wednesday night, his cousin, who used to live four doors down the road, came up and asked him to go on a trip with the Spanish students who always come to Buncrana every year to learn English. My sister was keeping one of them, so her wee boy came up and asked Oran if he would come along on a trip on the Saturday to the Ulster American Folk Park. And of course, Oran wanted to go, especially as his brother and his three elder sisters had all gone on these kind of trips over the years.

The children always enjoyed those trips. But Oran was only eight and I wasn't really happy to let him go, but I kept telling him that I would see. In the end, I told him he could go and on the Friday night he came in and said to me 'You'd better shake me hard in the morning.' He was always hard to wake up in the morning. So around 9 o'clock I was supposed to wake him, but I never woke until 9.00am myself and I thought for a split second that maybe I wouldn't bother, I'd just let him lay on, because I wasn't happy about him going really. Then I thought no, it wouldn't be fair on him. So, I woke him up and he was up like a shot. The minute I called him he jumped up. I remember the last thing just talking to him on the doorstep, telling him to watch out and watch his money, things like that. I just had a fear of letting him go, I thought that maybe he'd get separated from the rest of the group, that kind of thing. I was warning him to stay with the other boys and I was warning the boys to keep an eye out. The last time I saw him was with the others heading down to get the bus at school.

The day went by and I didn't think about Oran until about 3.30pm when I saw my two nephews who said that they were checking the Teletext for football results and had seen that there was a bomb in Omagh. One of the boys said to me 'That's where our boys will be now,' and I ran down the road to my sister's house to see for myself from the Teletext.

A bit later, I heard that there was five girls from Buncrana away on the trip as well and that one of them had phoned home and told her mother that there was a bomb and she was hysterical on the phone. So, when her mother told me that, I thought well the police will have them all in a safe place. But as time went on we knew for certain that they were in Omagh at that time. By the evening, all the neighbours were gathering outside the houses once they heard and the street was full of people.

We then heard that there were two Spanish students who were hurt, but we didn't hear that they were dead, just that they were hurt. At that point, we knew it was starting to get serious. It didn't look good at all and still there was no word where the other children might be. As the evening went on we were trying to get through to Omagh. The next message we got was that they were all safe and on their way home on the bus.

But, shortly after, we heard that this wasn't the right story. The five girls from Buncrana were safe and they were on their way home but we still didn't know about the others. About 6 o'clock I was at my sister's house and she got word that her wee boy Emmet was taken to hospital in Enniskillen to have shrapnel removed from his body and this really panicked me. But even then, we still didn't think the very worst because we were told that the bus would return to the town around 9 o'clock at night, so there was still a chance that the children might be safe. We went down there at 9.00pm to meet the bus but the driver told us that there was only sixteen Spanish students on the bus and all the rest were missing.

At that stage my husband and John McLaughlin and a few people from Buncrana left to go to Omagh to see if they could find out anything, so I just waited by the phone at my sister's house. The house was packed with people and everybody was gathered together waiting for any bit of information.

The next thing a policewoman phoned me and said that she had to talk with me and that because of policy she needed to talk with me on my own. I thought at that point that she was coming to tell me that Oran was dead, but she came down and took me into the small room on my own and said that two small boys were missing and one of them was Oran. At that stage, I just got hysterical and we were on the phone to the RUC in Omagh giving descriptions of Oran and Mickey. My husband rang from Omagh around 12 o'clock that night and said that they were at the Leisure Centre waiting, but there was still no word. He was saying 'Don't worry, I'll find our wee man, I'll bring him home.' But as the night went on and on there was still no word and we were starting to fear the worst. At the back of your head, you were thinking well maybe he was unconscious somewhere and someone had taken him in. I kept thinking this for ages.

About I would say 6.30 or 7.00 in the morning I was sitting at my sister's house which is only four doors down and I was sitting looking up at the McLaughlin's house and I could see all these people hugging each other, and I said to my sister 'You know there's something going on, they've got news of some sort.' She ran up there and quickly came back down with the news that wee Sean was dead. At that moment the phone rang and it was my husband, who asked me if I had heard the news. I said that I had heard about Sean being dead and it was then that he told me Oran was dead too. I just threw the phone. It was your worst nightmare come true.

For a wee while I thought I'd never even be able to go back to my own house because I didn't think I'd be able to deal with Oran's things without him. But somehow or other, I pulled myself together and went back to the house. I remember Mickey coming back from Omagh at 10.00 in the morning and the day of Sunday being a haze. On the Sunday night, my brother and his wife and a wee sister of mine took me up to the morgue at Omagh to see Oran's body. It was a makeshift morgue in the Army

Camp. Oran was dead from 3.30pm on Saturday but we didn't know he was dead until 7 o'clock on Sunday morning.

It was not until the Sunday night that I got to see his body. I remember going up to the morgue and it was so cold in there. At first, I didn't think they were going to let me see him, but eventually they did and oh, it was just something that I'll never ever forget, seeing him lying there. He wasn't so badly marked, but his hair was wet for some reason and it had changed colour. It was all dark and he had a big bruise on his cheek with a deep cut there as well. He had wee burns all over him at the same time but I suppose he wasn't half as bad looking as some of the victims. I don't know how I left him again that night to go home you know. I just came home and left him lying up in that morgue and it still haunts me that I didn't stay. I kept thinking and imagining him lying up there alone in the morgue on that Saturday evening.

We came home again that night and it was Monday night before we went back to Omagh to take the bodies home. It seemed that most of Buncrana came up in cars, up to meet in the wee Chapel of Rest here and see the three bodies of Oran, Sean and James Barker. All of their bodies were taken to this wee Chapel of Rest in Omagh and it was very late on Monday night before we went there. I'll always remember going down to that wee Chapel of Rest. It was terrible, the sight of those three coffins side by side. Some of my own girls were hysterical and they were screaming and wailing. But, I remember that night, on the way back from Omagh, with the three bodies, we were behind the three hearses and we went through Strabane.

There were people out standing with wee candles, and the closer we got to home, the more people were out holding a wee candle. It was incredibly moving. We took the bodies and went back here to Buncrana where the streets were just thick with men, women and children, holding a wee candle. I could see old friends just standing there screaming and crying. I was numb, just numb.

We brought him home to the house that night, which would have been the early hours of Tuesday morning and he stayed here until Wednesday. People from all religions came, along with politicians. Even the prime minister came. We had politicians from Protestant and Catholic communities, including Sinn Fein, Gerry Adams, Martin McGuiness and David Trimble all of whom came to the funeral. The crowds went on for miles. The church was packed out, people couldn't get in and there were loudspeakers outside for people to hear the service.

At different times, say Oran's birthday, or Christmas, or wee school trips and the like, I get very angry at the thought of the people who did this just going about their business. As yet, there are people still at large who did this and they are known to the authorities.

To lose your own child is very hard, but I just keep thinking what if something like this happened to my other children and that's why I feel that the people who done this should be brought to justice. I used to pray for God to keep the children safe. Every day a wee prayer in my head to keep them safe from harm. But, after Omagh, I can't seem to pray.

We always talk about Oran. There's hardly a day goes by without him being mentioned in the house. I think they're all confused about it, especially my youngest boy who never met Oran. When we walk to the grave we'll take him and he thinks that's where heaven is. For him, the graveyard is heaven and that's where Oran is, along with a whole lot of other children buried there who died of sickness, or accidents over the years. He thinks these are Oran's friends and this is where they live. Oran's elder brother wouldn't go back into Oran's room so we changed and my husband and me are in it now.

Recently, I was watching Oran's friends outside and I went up to bed, lay down and cried. I was wondering what Oran would be like now, hanging about with his friends. Would he be tall or short: Would his hair have darkened and would he be into baggy clothes? And I just cried my eyes out.

There was many a time after he died when I would wake up in the morning and just didn't want to get out of bed. I wanted to lay there and not face anything or anybody. But then, I would think of the children and that makes you get up.

Sometimes this sadness just pours over you. Like he brought some sweets in the Folk Park before they went to Omagh, a wee jar of honeycomb. And he had eaten one of the wee bits of honeycomb, but wrapped it up again. This was how he left it on the bus when he got out. And we got that back, his wee sweets. He should have come back that evening with them, but didn't. We didn't get anything else back belonging to him, except a wee thing he had round his neck, that his sister had brought him home from Spain the week before. One of those necklaces with a wee Nike sign on. We didn't get his clothes, or his footwear, or anything. We never even got the watch he had on him.

Bleeding and swelling of the brain and a fractured skull, that's what he died from in the bomb explosion. They said he would have died, if not instantly, then near enough. But to this day, the inquest results have not satisfied me because of conflicting reports.

About a week after it happened, we had a letter from a young girl on Omagh who said she was with Oran and that he didn't die alone. She said she was with him and held his hand, but she also said that he was already dead when she got to him. She was there just after the explosion and worked in the street nearby. Apparently, she just ran to the scene and come on Oran who was lying there. She described him and said she held his hand, even when they covered him. She said there were people calling to her to let him die with dignity, but she continued to hold his hand. At the time she thought she'd wait with him until his Mummy arrived. We met up with her twice after and it was so hard listening to her describing it. Later we were told that a nurse was on the street that day and that she was talking to him and that Oran spoke to her. After believing he must have died quick and didn't know anything, I started to think the worst, which is that he knew what was going on around him. I want to think that he didn't know anything. So when we were told that this nurse talked to him and he told her he wanted her to phone his Mummy and gave her our phone number, I was in a terrible state. But later on, one of the priests got it investigated and went to the RUC who said to dismiss the story because it didn't add up. Nevertheless, it was always in the back of my mind.

We didn't get the results of his death until almost two years later and that was just before the inquest. The reports were sent to our doctor here in Buncrana and she read it out to us, listing all the injuries he had suffered. He had a broken leg, broken ribs and a number of other wee injuries. It's funny, we knew from his death certificate that he had a fractured skull and bleeding and swelling of the brain, but when I heard then about the broken leg and broken ribs, that seemed to bother me even more.

Oran's body was number 15. The Counsel for the Coroner asked one of the policemen to describe how he found Oran. The policeman said that he came across a wee boy of about eight to ten years old and that his hair was still on fire, but that he was dead. And when the Counsel asked him to identify who that boy was, he replied that it was body number 15, Oran Doherty.

I still worry that Oran was talking and that he was alert to what was going on around him, even though I hate to think it and try not to. The thought that he did ask for me and I was fifty miles away is too much. I just want to think that he didn't know anything.

Kevin Skelton

Kevin Skelton is interviewed at the Omagh Victims Group Office in Omagh. He lost his wife Philomena Skelton (39) in the bomb. Kevin was the first person I interviewed.

My wife was a homebird. She spent most of her time at home looking after the family. I would have been the one that was out and about the most. She went shopping twice a year, Christmas and August to get the kiddies the school uniforms before they went back to school. That's the only time she went shopping. I would get the groceries every week, whilst she stayed at home knitting. That's basically all she did, full-time knitting. She was a great knitter, always doing different types of jumper. Yes, knitting and looking after the family, that would have summed her up.

We had four children and were a few days short of twenty years married. I met her in 1973 and we got married in 1978, on 31st August, a day before her twentieth birthday. Our first daughter was born on 28th August 1979, then, my son was born two years later. Some ten months later my second daughter was born and then my youngest daughter Shauna was born two years after that.

I was the one that was out all the time. I refereed football and did that most of the week. When I'd come home in the evening from work, my dinner was ready. I would eat my dinner, lift my kitbag and then be away to referee a match. And when I'd come home at night my kit was ready for me the next evening. Clothes were the same for going to work, set out for me at the top of the stairs every morning and my lunchbox was made. I couldn't have boiled an egg, she done everything. I was spoilt. Maybe that's being selfish, I don't know, but she was happy like that.

I normally worked on a Saturday and started work at 7 o'clock in the morning. I worked in a quarry, moving a lorry. I was in every morning at 7.00am and drew a load of tar. That particular Friday night, I had a sore back all day and when I came home from work I said to the wife 'I'm not going to work tomorrow with this back, I'm staying at home.' So I didn't go in. But about 8.30am the door got a thump and it was the boss man, knocking for me to do a load of tar. He said there would only be one load, which meant I'd be home fairly early. I was home around 12.15pm, and that's when the wife said we were going to Omagh to get things for the kiddies to go back to school. There would be uniforms and bits and pieces to get.

We arrived in Omagh at exactly 1.55pm and I know that because I parked my car in the front of the Royal Arms Hotel. In 1997 and 1998, she had brought a child from an orphanage in Romania, for a holiday to our home. The first year was for a fortnight and the second year was for three weeks and he went back on the Sunday before the 15th. But, that particular Saturday I had promised the child that I would write to Romania, and I know I was in Omagh at 1.55pm because I had to wait for five minutes for Travelcare (the travel agency) to open. I had gone in there to price a flight to Romania and afterwards I came up the street and went into Wattersons, a clothes shop, to find my wife, but she had left. So, I crossed over and found her in a shop called Tylers where she was looking for a pair of brown shoes for the daughter. I came out of there and I noticed a traffic warden who said that there was a bomb scare and that we would have to move on down the street. He said that a suspect bomb was at the Courthouse and that we would have to move. I moved my car from the front of the Royal Arms round to the car park at the back and came back on to the main street again. We were then moved on down the road and went into a wee confectionery shop beside Woolworths, where you get pencils and pens and different things for kids going back to school. We still hadn't got the shoes.

The police came in and asked us to move further on down the road, so naturally we moved on down. Nobody at the time seem too worried and I said to the wife that maybe we had better go home. She said that once we had got the shoes we would go home and then we went into a shoe shop opposite. Me and the wife and the youngest daughter crossed the street and Tracey, and my other daughter Paula, were round that area at the same time as well. We crossed over the road and by this stage I was fucking knackered running around looking for a pair of shoes. There's two parts to the shop she was in, where you step down from one part into the other. Tracey went down to the lower part and my wife and Shauna were standing beside the door. At that point, I said that I was going next door to a shop which sold ornaments and wee bits and bobs. I have a habit of walking around such shops looking. So I walked out and into this shop and I was halfway down the shop, just about to go back because I thought she would need money for the shoes, and then, bang! The bomb went off.

Now I would have been about six feet away from it when it went up. The front of the ornament shop just blew in and I was pulled out with it. The shop the wife was in was totally obliterated, blown right in. I can see it now, years down the line. I saw the explosion travelling down the street, bouncing off each building. Where one would blow in the next one would blow out. Shops fell in like a pack of cards and disintegrated like something out of a Hollywood film. The blast sucked up the whole street. First dive I made was into what was left of the shop my wife was in. I found her laying face down in the rubble. I tried for a pulse, but I couldn't find any. I couldn't find Shauna and I couldn't see the other two. I thought Shauna was buried underneath her mother. I don't know what I did in those immediate minutes, but I knew the first fireman I saw and I'd refereed him on many occasions at football. He came in, lifted her arm and then just dropped it down. I knew then that she was dead. Next the police came in and tried to move everybody out. They were on about another bomb at that particular stage but I didn't give a shit about another bomb. All I cared about was finding my daughters. I couldn't get to them.

It was thirty minutes or so that passed before I went back into the shop and it was then that I found Tracey, kneeling at her mother's side. A girl of sixteen years of age on her knees trying to find life in her mother. I knew she was alive but the youngest still hadn't been found. I found Paula shortly after that too. It was two hours before we found Shauna. A lady who was there gave me a brandy to settle me down and as I came out, there was a guy I didn't know, who shouted from the far side of the street 'Do you have a ginger-haired daughter?' I said yes and he told me that she had been taken to hospital. I took off to Omagh hospital and got there just when they were getting ready to take her to another hospital by helicopter. The whole side of her face had been blown in, but thank God she was alive. For those two hours, if I live to be 100, I will never forget them. Running about not knowing whether people were alive or dead and the smell of burning flesh.

In this country, there's conflict between Catholics and Protestants, but that day in Omagh, in the cries I heard from 3.10pm nobody came along and asked if you were Catholic or Protestant. The blood was all the one colour running down the street, and the screams of pain all sounded the same. I can't understand the mentality of the people who would plant a bomb like that, in the middle of a busy town. It does not take brave men to do that.

The next time I got to see my wife was at 10 o'clock on the Sunday morning. We spent all night at the Leisure Centre which had been set up like a command post. The people that were there had loved ones missing and most of them I knew. There were lists going up for Omagh Hospital, lists going up for Enniskillen Hospital, lists going up for Dungannon and lists going up for Belfast. Every time a list went up people ran to see if their loved ones names were on it. I didn't run. I knew that she was already dead, and it was 10 o'clock on the Sunday morning when I was taken to the Army Camp to identify her. My daughter was taken to hospital and my brothers and their wives went to stay with her. The next day, I had to do the hardest thing, which was to go and tell Shauna that her mother was dead. But, the strange thing was that she already knew.

The thing that saved me was that the glass was sucked out of the shop I was in. If it had been blown in, then I'd have been cut in two. Had the blast been seconds earlier,

I'd have been going into the shop where my wife and daughter were. My wife took the full force of the blast and saved my youngest daughter in the process.

The amount of people that came to the house was unbelievable. I went outside on the Tuesday to the driveway at 4 o'clock in the evening and the next time I went into the house was 12 o'clock at night. People were continually coming and shaking your hand. They came in their thousands from all over Ireland, all parts and all denominations. How I got through it, I don't know, that's a question I can't answer. How you stand that length of time and hold yourself together, I do not know.

My daughters Paula and Tracey didn't do too bad, but my son was not that good. He never saw his mother from the night before. He kissed her goodnight and that was the last time he ever saw her. Her coffin couldn't be opened because she was that badly damaged. He would have been sixteen, still a young lad and very close to his mother. If his mother was cleaning the windows inside, then he would have been doing them outside.

At the Army Camp a tent was set up which was where the dead were brought. My wife was killed on the Saturday and we didn't get her home until Tuesday. When I identified her I couldn't see anything wrong with her face, but maybe that's because I saw only what I wanted to see, I don't know. But, on the morning we went to take her home, I went out into the car and I said to my mother not to be surprised if we weren't able to open the coffin. Whether there was something in my subconscious from what I'd seen before I don't know, but when I went to pick her up from the undertakers I was told that the coffin couldn't be opened because she was too badly damaged.

The funeral was on the Wednesday and I had never seen anything like it in my life. The amount of people was unbelievable. There were busloads from all over Ireland. I remember feeling that I didn't seem to be getting anywhere. You seem to hit nothing but a brick wall and then you just go along with the flow.

At that particular time there were people like Tony Blair and Bill Clinton coming to Omagh to meet the families and we were very vulnerable to manipulation. We were promised everything at the time, but years down the line and the help hasn't materialised. We hear a lot about what happened on that particular day and what didn't happen and if the security forces on both sides of the border had done their job how that bomb would never have come in. It's a very hard pill to swallow.

My daughter who was injured made sure I got on and did things. If it weren't for her and my mother, I don't really think that I would be here today. I was left in a position where, because the wife did every thing, I couldn't boil an egg. I had to start and learn how to cook. I didn't know how to put on the washing machine. I dyed everything about the house. I washed clothes for the kiddies and the white blouses would have come out pink or blue, everything was dyed. With the help of my mother, I just battled on, but then my health started to suffer. I finished up at the hospital for three weeks and having my gall bladder removed, which was down to the stress.

What also helped to keep me going was the Romanian exchange. I had taken the child back six days before my wife died and afterwards thought that there was no way I could bring a child back again. But I did. In the summer and October of 1999 I went to Romania to adopt a girl and

I have been back to Romania seven times since. The children I met during those visits have been back here twelve times since 1997. This has definitely helped to keep me going. There have been many mornings when I have thought of putting a shotgun under my chin and pulling the trigger. But then I think about what my girls and son have been through. My family and Romanian family give me a reason to get up in the morning. Some of the families were lucky in one respect, which is that they weren't on the street when the bomb went off. Maybe that's being cynical, but they didn't see the scenes that I did and they were lucky not to have seen it. Nevertheless, they still had to go and identify their loved ones and nobody can prepare you for that.

Victims want the truth and they want to know why their loved ones died, but so far we have got nothing. I feel that I'd be doing my wife a disservice if I didn't try to bring to justice those responsible. If I don't speak for her then who will? She can't speak for herself and no politician here is going to speak for her either.

I feel very bitter. I have never been involved in politics of any type and have never been interested. But, because of it, I've got a life sentence which I will carry to my grave. There are nights I still can't sleep, and if I do sleep, I'll wake up and see people lying in the street. I can't even go and watch my favourite sport football, because I can't sit in a crowd. If I go to my local pub, I have to sit facing the door so that I can get out quick. That fear is always there. It never was before, but that fear is always there now, and it seems as if there's nothing I can do about it. That's how it feels anyway, like it won't go away.

Edith White

Edith White lost her husband Frederick (60) and son Bryan (27) in the bomb. Edith, who is quietly spoken, shows me photographs of Fred and Bryan. I talk to Edith at her home in Omagh where she makes tea and sandwiches for me. Edith refuses to accept the murder of Fred and Bryan and continues to this day to look for them.

On that particular day we had been back about twelve hours from our holiday and Fred and Bryan went into town to do some shopping, but I remained home to do housework, washing up, that sort of thing. Bryan said 'We're just off to town Mum, see you shortly', and that was the last time I saw them. They went together and Bryan had to drive because Fred wasn't allowed to after a brain haemorrhage. Not long after they had left, I heard this bang and I didn't know what it was.

I went out to the front and a neighbour said that a bomb had gone off in the town, but I thought at that point that Fred and Bryan would be well away from the explosion, because it sounded quite near. I came back in the house and waited for a while and then I thought I would go down the road to meet them. So I headed down the road and I walked to the area where it was shut off with a barrier, but I saw nothing. I asked somebody if there were any injuries but it was thought that there wasn't that many. This would have been sometime between 3.00 and

3.30pm. I walked back home and I tried the phone, but it was cut off and it was at that point that I started to get concerned, wondering why they were not back or had contacted me because they knew I would be worried. I don't know what happened much after that. I ended up at the County Hospital but how I got there, I don't know. I remember being at the Leisure Centre as well but I don't know how I got there either. I don't remember that at all. I remember somebody saying to me at some point 'Oh Fred's out there' and I asked the person who said it to ask Fred to wait by the desk for me while I continued to look for Bryan, but then I discovered that it was his brother.

My next recollection is what must have been that night when there were a number of folk who arrived here at the house. On the Sunday morning I remember seeing a lot of people sleeping on the floor in the lounge and I couldn't work out why. They were relatives. I think the doctor came to see me about midday on the Sunday to tell me what had happened. The next thing I recall is somebody telling me to go to bed for a while which is what I did.

After a short time the minister came in, sat on the side of the bed and talked for a while and he said 'We're bringing Fred and Bryan home', and this was in the dark of the night. I think that was on the Monday. I don't remember getting back here from the Leisure Centre and I don't have any recollection of what was said. I don't even know exactly how long Fred and Bryan [were] in the house. I think I was just walking around looking for them not taking any of it in.

Even though it's years later I can't accept that they are gone, maybe that's what keeps me going, I don't know. You see, I just can't accept they are really gone, because I don't understand why they had to be murdered. I know it sounds stupid to say that but I still think it can't be possible. I still go out in the car looking for them, thinking that they must be somewhere. Whenever I see a black Ford car I look to see if it's the number-plate of Fred's car. Their toothbrushes and everything are in the rooms just as they left them. The toothpaste is exactly as they left it and Bryan's room is exactly how he left it. I change the sheets regularly as if he's there. His diary is still lying by the bed. It helps me to keep it there. I've never been to counselling because I don't see what use it would be if they did not know Fred or Bryan. But, I'm also a private person. We were just a very normal family. The three of us were very close. We didn't socialise that much, we went on holidays and just stuck to our own activities. It wrecks your life and I think if I accept it then I just would not be able to cope. I need to be able to block it out as best I can and say that it can't have happened. It's important not to change. But I must say as time goes on it gets harder to think it hasn't happened. Sometimes the anger builds up and I have a cry to myself, but then I try to distract myself by doing something else.

Bryan and Fred were easy-going and easy to live with. Fred had a brain haemorrhage in 1989 and he retired from a job in the Accounts Department of the Western Board (education). After the brain haemorrhage he couldn't work at accounts any more, so he left and was just around the house. The garden and bits and pieces in the house would occupy him and then there were various organisations that he was in. Bryan was twenty-seven when he was murdered. He also did jobs around the house and did his own thing. He was a part-time student studying business and horticulture and worked as well in Strabane. He'd just got a new job there which he was about to start. I don't know what he really wanted to do but he enjoyed his life. He had a girlfriend and we keep in touch. Bryan studied in York for three years and then he came back to work. I also have a daughter, but the loss of Fred and Bryan is never mentioned. I don't know if it's because she finds it too hard or wants to close it off, but I'm not willing to let the murder of Fred and Bryan die down. I go to the support group and I want a public enquiry. The people who did this should be made accountable for what they did. They should not be walking free and I won't let it drop.

During that first week I couldn't tell whether it was dark or light. I remember there were a couple of other folk here and I can still see people coming through the door, but I'm not sure who they were. I would say people were here until the funeral. Although the coffins were in the house I can't remember much about it. I know there were thousands of people turning up here, but I was in a complete daze, utterly lost. I was on strong tablets, a really heavy dose and I was on them for quite a while. I can remember being in the church and staring at two coffins and then standing in the graveyard. Things were taken out of my hands at that point and I wasn't up to anything. You feel your life is at an end and there's nothing to live for, that's how I constantly feel.

You go from day to day and that's the best you can do. I don't go to church now, but I go to the graveyard twice a day, do housework and am involved in the support group. I just have that feeling that I have to go to see where they are. Most of the other folk who lost loved ones have somebody else in the house, husband, wife, or children, whereas I've been left on my own. I had a brother but he died from meningitis.

I don't like the solitude because you tend to dwell on things more. I have to push myself all the time and particularly at times of the year such as birthdays, Christmas and Easter which are particularly bad. Fred was very active in the garden at Easter but I get somebody to do the garden now, and I admit that I find it hard to see somebody else doing it.

Some of Bryan's friends still keep in touch with me, in fact one lad who was his best friend calls quite often. I also see Fred's friends now and again. But, there are some people who don't like the thought of me pushing for an enquiry. Some have cold-shouldered me, but I don't care too much about that. We had friends we used to see quite a lot of before, but they don't come now.

Things are more or less the same for me all these years on. I get up, dressed, go to the graveyard, come home, do the housework, go back to the graveyard again and I try to do a bit of reading or work in the garden. Most of the reading is of reports and documents about Omagh. I'm trying to build up a list of reasons, why I want a public enquiry. I've not spoken to any journalists at all. I do try and read other things but I can't focus properly. I read last night and at 4 o'clock again this morning, but if you asked me what I was reading about I could not tell you. It's hard to concentrate and I know that since this happened my memory has just gone completely. I'm on tablets, but I had what they call a 'downer' a couple of weeks ago where I just did not want to leave the house, get out of the bed or anything. I had terrible headaches so I went to doctor and my blood pressure was right up, and I'm waiting for blood test results now. I don't really sleep that well and I have nightmares. If I get four hours a night I'm lucky.

The unanswered questions annoy me very much because I feel it's been a case of delaying action as long as possible in the hope that we will either give up or die away. Some have left the group. I think it's been important to talk with others who have been through the same experience and to see how they are coping and support each other. In the early stages I was very cautious, but then I gave it a go. It's been helpful in that it has led to a lot of researching into the bomb and what happened that day, but we are not really that much further on.

A lot of obstructions have been put in the way of trying to find out what happened. I have a number of questions about the security that day, and the longer they remain unanswered the more I want them answered. There was a huge problem with security because if that had been as it should, then I wouldn't have lost my husband and son.

I remember the holiday, we went to Aberdeen and were just travelling around. My daughter had been at Aberdeen University and we thought we would go and look around there for a while. The year before 1997, I had gone to Aberdeen on my own and Fred and Bryan remained at home because they were going to the flower show, which I wasn't interested in. So when it came to 1998 we all went, for six days, travelling by car and staying at bed and breakfast. We also had friends over there. And when we came back Fred and Bryan went into town to get some food, which we could have done without. Normally we would have never gone into town on a Saturday because we did our shopping on a Friday, and Bryan would have been out somewhere.

Afterwards when all the politicians came here I didn't have anything to do with it. I didn't go to town when Bill

Clinton and Tony Blair came here either. I stayed at home. Some politicians came here but I can't remember what they said. When people went, I suppose I tried to carry on as normal. But I was out searching for Fred and Bryan practically every day because I thought this just could not have happened. I still go out and trace the route they took. Of course, when I come back it's the empty house again. I was married for thirty-two years up until Fred was murdered. I worked in teaching at the Omagh College but left after Fred had his brain haemorrhage because I didn't want to leave him here on his own. He was told not to climb anything and I remember coming home and there he was on an extended ladder, trying to continue as he always did. I used to teach Business Studies to sixteen to twenty-year-olds and had been in teaching all my life, well for twenty-eight years. I am more short-tempered and cynical now and certainly not as energetic. You can't go on as before. I go from day to day. I concentrate on the house now, it tends to take up most of my time, but by the same token I think why worry about it, who's here to see it? I would never have a lodger here either, I would see that as disrespectful to Fred and Bryan. You see much of what I do relates to what they would have thought and done and I'm always asking myself what they would have said. I have those conversations in my head all the time. I've felt the same ever since they were murdered, which is like having a tremendous weight on top of me.

I can't really enjoy myself any more either. When Fred and Bryan were here life was completely different. I belonged to a few organisations like Women's Institute and the church group. But now I can't go out with a number of people because I feel I shouldn't be with groups enjoying myself when Fred and Bryan are not here. There's a considerable guilt there. Now the house is now the only place I feel comfortable and when I go out I get back to the house as quickly as possible. I suppose it's the routine that gives me a bit of security now, although I was never like that before. Then I was quite spontaneous, I would often just take off and do things. I think medication dulls you down as well and I've had a fair bit of that.

I would like to see those who murdered my husband and son brought to book, but it's also important to look at the security arrangements that day because if they had been right, then lives could have been saved. I want an admission of that and I want to know why. You can't sit there when your husband and son have been murdered and do nothing about it. It would be neglecting them to do nothing. But I know there are a lot of powers-that-be who would rather this went away now and who think that Omagh should be over and done with by now. People have said to me it's been years now, it's over and done with so get on with your life, but I can't. I do think though that on the other hand, I have also softened towards people more and that I have more time for them. There's no doubt about it that if I had been living the life I did before, I wouldn't have met so many people. I am in touch with a lady who lost her daughter in the Enniskillen bomb quite often. She also lost her husband a couple of years later and she seems to think it was the stress. People who haven't been through that can't relate to it to the same extent. That's the way I see it, this is my life now and this is how I will stay. I go to Castlederg for my shopping which is about twenty miles away. I haven't been into Omagh since the bomb and I don't intend to. I hate the name of the place now. I don't want to see new buildings that have been built on top of my husband's and son's blood. I'll never go back there.

Bridie Marlow

Bridie Marlow runs a pub in a small village just outside Omagh. I talk with her in her living room about her daughter Jolene who was seventeen. Bridie talks openly about Jolene and has had a CD of songs performed by Loreto Grammar School made as a tribute. She gives me a copy of the CD to keep and we talk over tea for an hour about Jolene, the bomb and the aftermath. Bridie has another daughter, Nikki, who was seriously injured in the bomb.

Jolene was a very fun-loving, sporty, athletic and academic girl who loved life and was my friend. She went through all her grammar exams a year early and did her Eleven Plus before she was ten. She left primary a year early and went to grammar school and got all her GCSEs and had just taken her A Levels and was waiting on her results. We got the results the day after her funeral. She got two Bs and a C which would have taken her into Jordanstown to do physiotherapy for her degree.

I can remember all that day. In the morning, Jolene got up and got ready for work as usual, she had a part-time job in Omagh and we took her to work. We came home, went to mass, and then took the two young boys to football because they had a match. After the match they came home and had food. Nikki, my other daughter, had been baby-sitting two weeks beforehand and she had a bit of money saved up so she had planned to meet Jolene in Omagh to buy tickets for a concert. My sister was over from England so she and my mother arrived here and she gave my mother a lift to Omagh. They were dropped off in Omagh about 1.30pm. Nikki brought the tickets and arranged to meet Jolene who switched her normal dinner hour with some of her friends at work to meet Nikki.

The first I heard of the bomb was when this wee lad came into the bar and said that there had been an awful explosion in Omagh and that people had been killed. It just never dawned on me about my own two. The lad said that it had been on a newsflash and at this stage it must have been 3.30-3.45pm, so I went down to my sister-in-law's house where Nikki was supposed to meet up with my mother and sister and there was no answer there. I rang the grocers where Jolene worked and there was no answer there either, but I kept trying and eventually I got talking to Jolene's first cousin who works there as well and asked him if Jolene was there. He said no that she was not back from lunch and I thought then that she wouldn't have been out for lunch for that length of time. I asked about the bomb in town, and he said it wasn't near where they worked, but that Jolene was on the opposite of the town. I asked him if he knew why she might be so long in coming back and he said the chances are that she has probably got caught up with the queues of people that had been pushed back and not allowed to cross the line. I was content enough for that at that point.

Then I thought that I would check the news and I reached over to get the paper and I was talking to my husband quite casually at this point who had just finished in the bar. I told him about the news that there had been a big bomb in Omagh and that I had been trying to get information about the girls, but I couldn't get any. And he said that we should to go to Omagh.

Even at that point, I still thought they would be alright. I was thinking that we would see the vast destruction in front of us, but that that would be it. I can also remember thinking on the way if it's not our girls killed in this bomb the chances are it would have to be somebody else's. I held on to the thought that it wouldn't be our two and that it would be somebody else's.

We got to Omagh and were diverted, but we parked up and were walking towards the devastation when for some reason I started crying, even though I had no idea that our two might be involved. We came to the line and all the destruction was in front of us but I have no recollection of what I saw at that particular moment. We went and asked a policeman about the situation who was crying and he said there were over twenty dead and hundreds injured. It was only then that it started to hit me that our two could be caught in this.

We met one girl who was friendly with Jolene and she was in a wheelchair with blood all over her hands and a bandage on her head. I asked her if she had any idea where Jolene was and she said 'Well she must be alright because I was talking to her before the bomb went off and she was further away from the explosion than I was'. We met up with my sister who went to collect Nikki and she said she had been to a nursing home or something where lists had been put up to find relatives. We found Nikki there and it was devastating. She was covered in blood from top to bottom. I came walking down the ward and it was her socks that I recognised her by. Her clothes were blown off and there were nurses working with her. She was in a terrible state asking where Jolene was and my aunt was in the bed beside her also asking where Jolene was.

At this stage I assumed that Jolene may have been one of the walking wounded who might have been taken to Derry or Enniskillen or somewhere. She was the type of girl who would have tried to help somebody else even if injured herself. I tried to comfort myself with that thought for hours thinking that's where she would be. Then we got word that Nikki had to be taken to another hospital, but we couldn't leave because we had to try and find out what had happened to Jolene. Eventually my sister and a good friend said that they would go with Nikki so we could stay.

It was about 4 o'clock in the morning before we found out she was dead. We were moved from the hospital to the Leisure Centre and they were drawing up lists all the time from the different hospitals identifying the injured in those hospitals and we were just kept updated with lists. When a list went up you just hoped that the name of your loved one would be on it. Jolene's name never appeared. Later that night a meeting was called where we were told that those whose names were not on the lists would possibly probably be dead. And about 4 o'clock somebody came in and said there were x amount of bodies in the mortuary set up at the Army Camp. I had to give a description of her to someone and a priest came to tell us that she was among those dead. My brother and sister went to identify her in the morgue and we had to come home.

All through that whole time we were in the Leisure Centre we kept in touch with the hospital where Nikki was at because we didn't realise how serious her injuries were. Her condition we were not told about until a week afterwards, when it turned out that things had been very much touch and go. We came home here about 6 o'clock in the morning and left about 9 o'clock to go and see Nikki. She had been in the operating theatre all night and we asked advice as to whether we should tell her the bad news about Jolene.

A chaplain in the hospital told us that Nikki had a lot of serious wounds and that as a worst case scenario she may lose her right arm. We asked him what to do and how the news might affect her. He said that she would probably know as soon as she saw me. And the first thing she asked was where Jolene was and we told her. She told us to go home and sort Jolene out and then to come back after that. But she was in total shock. We didn't find out until months later that Nikki never knew that Jolene was dead until she saw it on television in hospital. We spent every hour we could after the funeral and we stayed with her in the hospital and then on the tenth day she was transferred to Dundonald hospital where I spent six weeks sleeping on two armchairs beside her bed.

We saw Jolene when she was brought home here on the Monday and the funeral was on the Wednesday. On the first night of the wake there was a book of condolences opened from 3 o'clock that day to 11 o'clock that night and there was something like 1500-1600 names. I must say that it was shock that carried us through. People say you don't want anybody around you at a time like that but we did, and there was no choice in the matter. Most people were supportive and helpful, but it was the shock that took us through. You go onto a sort of automatic pilot. I don't know how others coped but that's what it was like for us.

Apart from that we had to bear up for Nikki's sake. The media were arriving here on the morning of the funeral but I refused to have anything to do with them. My youngest was only six. We were told we carried it through in a dignified way, but it was shock there's no doubt about it.

I can remember going around the wards meeting people who had been badly injured and I just had this urge to keep going from one person to the next asking how they were and it was only some time later that I realised that this was connected to shock as well. I was in that state for some time. We had three other children at that time who were six, nine, and eleven, who were boys, and not only had they lost Jolene, but Nikki was gone and my husband and myself were up at the hospital more than we were at home. It was only through the good support of my husband's family and friends that we got through that. I had counsellors visit me and I turned counselling down because I didn't like people telling me how to feel or warning me that tomorrow I would feel worse. When I want a counsellor I will ask for one. I found a lot of therapy in people writing to me and me writing to them. People who have suffered tragedies since I have written to, even if I didn't know them. I try to share my tragedy with them and talk with them about the experiences I have had. That's probably been the most therapeutic thing for me.

When Nikki came out of hospital and came home it was very difficult because we were trying to run a business as well. We had lots of people visiting and they came because they have a good heart, but it just became very wearing. It was a lot of hard work because Nikki needed a lot of care. She had nurses coming in to dress her injuries every day and I had to do all the personal things with her as well as keep the house going and keep the children at school, although I had a lot of help from the family as well. But it affects you because all this is going on in your house and you have very little control over it. I tried to distract myself with housework and doing the books for the bar. The impact was steady, although I feel that we dealt with it very very well. When I look back at the things we had to cope with, I think we coped very well, because we could easily have let everything slide and let it all go downhill.

At no time did myself or my husband become unbearable towards the children. We made a strong effort to keep up and you know we still talk about it to each other. But it not only affected us, it affected the community. Jolene was well regarded here, but all those people who knew Jolene have dwindled away and this has impact on your custom as well. So there are a whole range of ways in which this affects your life: a number of small details. Jolene was due to start University the September after she was killed. Every year since, I am constantly looking out for graduations thinking that should have been her. The children also say they wonder what Jolene would have been doing now. Jolene worked so hard to pass her qualifications and her life was so full at the time. She played sports for her school, for a club, for the parish and had a good social life all at the same time. I'm so glad I didn't stop her from having all those things. But it's also made me more angry as a person. There's no doubt about it, we've all done life sentences because of this.

Some years on we have the same loss and bear the same scars. I do worry about how it will impact on Nikki because she suffered so many injuries and she has been told she may suffer from arthritis at a very young age. But she shields my feelings and I shield hers. Nikki has written down her recollections of that day and I have read it. She has no clear memories of the street. The problem as well is that she can't seem to talk about things in the present tense, she finds it very hard and wants to know why she should do so. My aunt was badly injured as well and suffered two heart attacks before being moved to Belfast. It was touch and go but she has made a good recovery. Jolene died from the blast of internal bleeding and had bad injuries. If she had survived I don't know what her life would have been like because she suffered so many injuries. Nikki had a lot of injuries, from head to toe virtually, but Nikki was a big strong girl in comparison to Jolene. Nikki lost about half of the back of her calf and it was only because she had big strong sturdy legs that she didn't lose a leg.

I still feel Jolene's presence and that she's helping us and guiding us along, more so now than beforehand. That is the comfort we take from it. I try to explain to some people that you can look to your loved ones for help. I firmly believe that Jolene has helped us through many a crisis since and that maybe we would not have been able to cope with if she were here. You have to have experienced what I have to know what that means. If I had not lost Jolene I would just not have believed that. I find myself fussing less about things now, whereas before I would have fussed about this and that. Some of my friends have said how hard they are going to find it when their kids go off to University, but I would love to be in that position, yet I can understand it because before I was the same. Even after the tragedy I wouldn't let the kids out of my sight or let them go to Omagh.

There are some people who have treated us with the highest of regard. But there's a certain amount of people who feel that six years down the line and you shouldn't be talking about it, or think that we got a load of money out of this, which is untrue. So you get two sides of people, but I should say that a lot of people have been supportive.

One of the things with being associated with Omagh, is that unlike somebody who loses a loved one through an accident or an act of individual murder, when nobody remembers the time it happened or the date it happened, whereas in our case nobody will forget. Most people remember the date and what they were doing on that day. My brother was killed on a motorcycle but who will have heard about it? To me because of the tragic circumstances, I think that it's right that it should be remembered. People say to me does it bother you when it gets dragged up every year and I say no it doesn't and I don't think it can be dragged up often enough. The people out there who have forgotten are the people who need to be reminded.

Godfrey Wilson

I interview Godfrey at his bungalow in Omagh. His wife Ann stays in the kitchen unable to talk about the loss of their daughter Lorraine (15). I sit with Godfrey in his living room which is decorated with photographs. Lorraine can be seen horse-riding in one of the photographs. She looks confident and happy. The interview is punctuated with a number of pauses as the recollections continue to upset Godfrey. His youngest son also comes into the room and listens to what Godfrey has to say.

I lost my daughter Lorraine in the bomb. She was doing charity work that day along with her friend Samantha McFarland. I'd called her that morning because I thought that she had slept in instead of going to the Oxfam shop where she worked. Sure enough she was sound asleep in bed, which gives me a guilt complex because I woke her from her sleep to go to her death. That was the last I saw of her alive, when I woke her up. My other daughter, who doesn't live with me, phoned later that day and was up for a visit. Lorraine also phoned and said she was going to the town at 4 o'clock to see Denise who owed her some money. Denise would meet Lorraine and give her the money because she wanted to buy some new shoes to go back to school that afternoon.

We went into the town at 3 o'clock, myself, the wife,

Denise and my son, to give Lorraine the money but we were diverted from going up the main street because there was a bomb scare in the town. We went round the Northern bypass and came in the back of Boots chemist, thinking we would get into the town and get to the Oxfam shop that way. Denise went to find Lorraine in order to give her the money but couldn't get out onto the main street because the police stopped her. So we were turned home just after 3 o'clock.

We went home and it was there that we heard the bomb go off. My wife, who was on the phone to her mother, immediately said 'Lorraine's dead'. Why she said that we still don't know. Denise and my oldest son Garry rushed back into town to try and find Lorraine, hoping that she would be okay. They got to the local chemist shop and didn't realise that the body lying across the road from them was Lorraine. My wife and myself tried to get to the town in the car, but we met so many buses and taxis coming up with injured people that we had to divert and come home again. I went down on my bicycle and my youngest came with me. When we got there I was talking to Garry and Denise and they said there was no word of Lorraine. We decided to come home and check the hospitals and Denise phoned Enniskillen and Belfast etc. Myself, the wife and Garry went down to the local hospital and made enquires but could find no information about Lorraine.

When we got home we went straight to the Leisure Centre where they were keeping lists of people that were hospitalised. We also went to the local Health Centre to see if they had any information. From then on we sat in the Leisure Centre from 5 o'clock until 11 o'clock Sunday morning when we were taken to the local Army Camp to identify Lorraine. She was cut up with shrapnel and was soaking wet where the mains water had burst and Lorraine was lying in the water and this is how she was picked up and how we saw her. There was nothing done to tidy her up.

We went home then and I cried and cried and it didn't stop. It was a terrible time. We waited for Lorraine's remains to come home. There were so many other people destroyed and it took the mortuaries some time to deal with everybody and prepare them for burial. We didn't get Lorraine home until Tuesday evening and her funeral was on Wednesday. There were multitudes of people that came to the house. It was unbelievable, for days they just kept coming.

My wife had to get medical treatment to cope with it and we still try to battle on. I went back to work after fourteen weeks and found it very hard to cope with it. I had to try and get back to some normality, but normality wasn't coming to me because it was always in the media. There was always somebody enquiring into what happened and what we were doing.

We expected justice to be done and to date we haven't had it. We saw all the politicians on both sides of the community and in Britain and Ireland, the terrorists were still killing and destroying and we've been unsuccessful in getting justice. I feel very hurt that I have lost my daughter and that society has let us down. In the first place, the people who think they are doing something beneficial for Ireland are on the wrong track when they're destroying innocent lives.

Society as a whole has let us down with respect to

justice. The politicians were trying to show that they were going to take on responsibilities, but it was only public relations. They didn't want to be seen to be taking sides because of the cross community impact of the bomb. You had Protestant, Catholic, Mormon, Spanish and people from the South who were hurt by the politicians' PR.

I don't know what state I was in. Sometimes I felt jolly, but I can only put it down to being in a state of shock. I was greeting people at the door with a smile on my face. I knew I was doing it but I just couldn't help it. My mind was shattered. It must be the way the body reacts to keep you from going over the top. The living room, kitchen and bedrooms never emptied until the funeral.

I was standing at the front door and people were coming in groups of thirty or forty. It was nearly impossible to deal with it. When you saw the state of the carpet after the funeral you could tell how many were in here. There was one bloke who came to the door when I wasn't in and apologised for a member of his family who had been in the Republican Movement. This family member was 'lifted' as a suspect for the bomb, but was subsequently released. The chap at the door wanted me to know that he had no such affiliations with the Republican Movement, but I don't know what I would have done with him at that time if I had been there.

On the day of the funeral I just stayed close to the family. We rallied round each other to try and keep each other strong. I didn't take any tablets for the state I was in because I felt I had to keep up face for the rest of the family. But when I got to the graveside and laid Lorraine to rest, I just lifted my head and looked around me and the multitude of people just scared the hell out of me. I couldn't see any empty spot in the graveyard. People moved forward to shake my hand. I just had to get out of it. I asked a workmate of mine to help me back to the car. I went into a state of panic. When we got home, it was a sad and lonely house and I've been fighting it physically and mentally ever since. I don't think I can ever come to terms with what I have lost.

The local community opened the Trauma Centre and they sent a woman out to deal with us, but unfortunately even though the woman had experience of dealing with violence she had no experience with bereaved families and there was nobody else who did either. I went and put my name down for counselling and went down to the Centre. The chap sat there and listened to what I had to say. Four times I went down and I asked him what experience he had in dealing with traumatised people and he said he had none. The only experience he had was with alcoholics and nervous breakdowns. So I didn't go anymore. It wasn't helping me.

I went back to work, but I was off a lot with depression and just didn't feel capable of doing the job. The company who I worked for decided to send me to counselling and they sent me to another bloke. I said that I needed to talk with somebody who has lost in their life and knew how I felt. So they put me in contact with a man who had lost his son in a cot death and his other daughter had committed suicide. It helped me to talk to him. But talking with you here today, I feel that I haven't moved on much when I start digging into my heart and soul.

I tried to get on with my life, but spent most of my time crying. I ended up with ulcers in my eyes. I did attend a few meetings for bereaved families and talked to them about my experiences because I felt I had to let people know what had happened to me. Anything that came up such as television interviews I attended because I felt that I wanted the world to know about what I had lost. But when I saw how the interviews were put together I felt like I was being used.

There was a particular time during a well-known chat show when the presenter asked me who was strongest me or the wife. I just stated that I couldn't stop crying because I was so hurt and that I had cried for nine months. The woman asked my wife if she thought I was a wimp crying all the time and when I saw it on the television, I just felt terrible. I was at work and I got a phone call to say there was a show and they wanted me to be on it that evening. We had to fly out that day at 6 o'clock. So I went to the supervisor and asked for a half day, rushed home got cleaned up, went to the airport and at the end of it all I felt used. It was just devastating. At the time though I thought I was doing the right thing.

We created the support group because we felt that the trustees were treating us like second-class citizens. We weren't after the money, but we felt it was wrong when injured people seemed to be more entitled to money than the bereaved and the reason we created the group is because the injured are entitled to every penny they get, fair enough, but they have an argument with the state which entitles them to compensation for their injuries, whereas the bereaved families didn't have that.

I've been to Court four times and they say I'm not a traumatised person, they define me as a bereaved person and not a traumatised person. I can't tell the difference. The government knew that the bomb was coming into the town and they did nothing. I've paid my dues all my life. There's a police force out there, it's a garrison town and the government are responsible for protecting the lives of civilians, which they didn't do. And with me paying my dues to the government all my life I feel that I've been let down.

I feel that I'm still sitting here five years down the line no further on. My family and myself have paid a real price. I think you've caught me on a bad day. I feel resentful today, a bit emotional. There's days we just can't seem to cope. You see Lorraine was such a lovely girl, a homely girl. At the same time she was very outgoing. She went horse riding and raced go-karts and lived life to the full. Swimming, discos or whatever, she was out there enjoying her life. But she was such an important part of the family, and when you start thinking about it and what should have been, then it's very hurtful.

People don't realise what goes on behind closed doors in a situation like this. There have been attempts in the family to take life, which we have had to deal with. Trying to take your own life because of an act that other people have imposed, it's demented. But for one family member finding out in time we would have been attending another funeral. The kids do try and put it to the back of their minds, but if they try and talk about it then it becomes shattering to them. There has been problems around suicide threats...on two occasions. To find a loved one trying to kill themselves, people don't realise what you have to deal with. You're trying to be as strong as you can for your family and then there's Ann and me sat up at night wondering if someone is taking tablets to end it all.

You don't want to be looking in every minute and

checking because that only makes someone feel more guilty. You see this is another problem, which is that as victims we can't seem to get away from. It's there all the time.

We've had to fight to get everything, even a memorial garden with flowers. They built a community house afterwards but nobody came to the victims to ask where they wanted it, so where did they build it? They built it on top of the bomb site. The thing about victims, is that we feel the politicians have used us for PR purposes. When you phone them for six months arguing with them and asking for an interview, they eventually come to do it, but the only reason is to say that they have talked to the victims.

We've talked to politicians and none of them have come back to us. The media seems to be our battlefield. It's the only spot we can turn to that will listen. We've sent letters to politicians to come and meet the bereaved families, and the only time they did was when elections were due and again it was for PR. Once elections were over that was it.

It's important to see what happens to people in situations like this. People keep saying why don't you move on, it's time to move on, but that's very easy to say when your family grows up and you've no tragedy like this clinging to you. It's nice to see young girls passing their driving test and moving on to better things, but the problem is when I see them moving on, I think about Lorraine and she's still fifteen. Because of the ignorance of others, our daughter won't be doing those things.

Patricia McLaughlin

Patricia lives in Buncrana. She lost her son Sean (12) on a student visit to Omagh. Patricia lives two doors away from Bernie Doherty who also lost her son Oran on the trip. Patricia talks quietly and openly about Sean. She is angry about the loss of Sean and this is evident when we talk. We sit in the living room and talk for about an hour.

Sean was a lively, lovely lad. He liked playing football with his mates and cycling and doing things that young boys do. He played football for his local club. Sean had gone on these trips for the previous two years, it had become a summer event. It never occurred to me that they were going into Omagh town though. I didn't know they were actually going into the town.

We had been out for the day and we came back. I went down to the town here to get the groceries and one of the women said that there had been a bomb in Omagh and that a bus from Buncrana had been caught up in it.

At first I asked if it was a crowd of old people who had gone there on a day out. It never occurred to me at all that Sean would be involved. I left the town with groceries and came home and on my way in the woman next door came out about 4 o'clock. She was crying and said 'Is Sean alright?' and I said 'of course, why wouldn't he be?' She said the bus with the children on from the town had been caught in the bomb.

I knew they had gone to the Folk Park, but I didn't know they had gone on to Omagh. The Folk Park is a mile or two outside of Omagh. I didn't think that the children would be going into the town to get sweets and things. It just never occurred to me.

I came indoors and put on the news to see what was happening and then everybody in the houses here seemed to come out. I saw Bernie (Doherty) a couple of doors down and she was very upset. I kept saying to her that they would be alright. And she kept saying that they were not going to be alright.

So it carried on and we got news then of two boys that were with them, Bernie's nephew and his friend, that the four of them had gone together and their parents were sent for because they were very badly injured. The parents had to go straight away and I kept saying that we would be sent for next but that everything would be alright; that we would have to go to Enniskillen Hospital or one of the other hospitals where people were being sent to.

We were on the phone and talking to the RUC (Royal Ulster Constabulary) and they were trying to get information for us. Along with that we were watching television for any other news. We didn't go to Omagh at that point. We didn't think there would be any point because everything was in a mess and it was obvious that there was no way that you were going to see or find out anything. So we waited on and we were told that the bus would be coming back that night at 9 o'clock with the rest of the kids.

We still thought there was a chance that the boys would be on it. We went to the school and I think it was at that stage for some reason that I felt there was a good chance that they weren't coming home. I got on to the bus and the parish priest was on there and a sergeant and the driver and we knew the driver and I asked if anybody had seen Sean and Oran and nobody had. I knew then that was it. That was the end.

My husband and Bernie's husband decided at that point that they would go to Omagh, so they left with two other men and went down. And me and Bernie came home.

I would be going to her house and she would come to mine to see if there was any news and it was about an hour after the men left that the RUC kept phoning to try and find out what Sean was wearing and if he had any identification marks or anything on him which would allow them to identify him.

The later it got, the more they kept phoning and the calls were getting closer together. One of the doctors from the town here heard what was going on and phoned through to try and use that bit of extra authority to get more information, but she didn't get any further than us. They just asked her the same kind of questions. I knew that by asking the same kinds of questions they must have had a body that they wanted to identify.

My husband was phoning me regularly as well, but he was also visiting the four or five hospitals where the injured were sent to. They started with the closest and carried on down towards Omagh. He told me that when he got to Omagh, they went to the Leisure Centre where there were sheets of paper with everybody's name on letting relatives know where the injured had been sent. But the later it went on the worse it got. About 7.30am he was told there were two boys that resembled the descriptions of Oran and Sean.

Sean was very badly disfigured and so he couldn't be easily identified. John then came back and his family and my family were here all night. They had heard that Sean was missing. John and the others got back about 10 o'clock in the morning. So then of course they had to bring Sean home, but we were told that the earliest they could release the body would be Tuesday. That meant Sean would be on his own from Saturday until Tuesday and it was at that point that all hell broke loose. I just went crazy. I couldn't accept that he would be alone for that length of time.

A good friend of ours phoned the RUC to see if there was any way at all that they could hurry the post-mortem along and get Sean released earlier, or if we could go and see him. We got permission then to go up Sunday night to view him at the mortuary. So me and Bernie went up and they were just out of the post-mortem at that stage. I think at that point you don't actually see things right. But we had to go, because until I saw Sean, I still thought that he was going to come home.

He was released on the Monday and there must have been thirty to forty cars that went up to Omagh and we brought him back. I insisted on Sean's coffin being opened and I was told it couldn't be but I insisted and of course they had to do a lot of work to cover up the injuries. The state of his face meant that it took a lot longer than they thought it would and it was very late when we left, sometime in the early hours of Tuesday morning.

The crowds of people on the route were unbelievable. From when we left through all the towns it was on both sides of the street and those people had been waiting ages because we left much later than we were due to leave. But they were still standing. And when we got to the bottom of the town here there were thousands stood at the side of the road.

The people visiting this house queued right down the road and round the corner in two lines all day and all night. Sean was here in the front room and they would come in on one side of the room and go out on the other all day and all night. It never stopped. It was a distraction but at that stage I was somewhere else, you just didn't know what was going on or what was happening. I didn't want anything to sink in, so I was blocking everything out.

I knew there were people there and my hand was sore and swollen from shaking hands. I had two rings on and I had to take them off because the hand was swollen and the rings were cutting in to me. For two days after I couldn't bend my hand at all. Close relatives and friends stayed all night as well. I had never seen as many people in my life, I don't know where they came from, but they arrived from all over the place and were of all ages.

After the funeral I just seemed to be in a lull, but all my family were here, even the ones from America and England and they were very protective. But I just felt totally numb, along with anger. I don't think things sunk in properly for a month or six weeks. John would not talk to me about it, but he spoke to other people.

The kids had a very bad time of it, they were desperate.

The youngest boy who was only seven, he couldn't cope at all. He had nightmares and he wouldn't go into Sean's room. One of my daughters insisted on sleeping in Sean's bed, but the boy wouldn't go into the bedroom at all. He slept in my room for months and had recurring nightmares. Then he would get very angry and very aggressive and his personality would change overnight. At other times he was just completely quiet. He also became a disruptive influence at school and was disturbing everyone else in the class. 'That went on, but then it calmed down and I thought things were getting better until one night I went to see some friends and I got a phone call from someone in the family who had taken tablets. When you think things can't get any worse.

I saw a counsellor a few times but I was more angry than anything else. The kids tried it but they would talk more to me or their friends. I have two sisters that lost two kids and my husband had a sister who died when she was twenty-three and a brother who died when he was not even three, so I had plenty of my own family to talk to who knew what we were going through. I need this more than somebody looking at me and then asking 'How do you feel today?' and I would say 'how the fuck do you think I feel today?' In the end, I said that if I needed counselling I would ask for it.

Along with that there was the media to contend with, although I have to say that most of them were very good. They were camped outside the house on the other side of the road but they weren't disrespectful to be fair. Unless I spoke to them, they didn't bother me. I can't exactly remember what I said to them. The attention was overwhelming. Also I've never seen so many 'big nobs' in all my life, but at that time, I must say, it didn't make any difference who came here.

We used to go down to Omagh to see the support group, but after a while I didn't feel that it was for me. I had to try and get on with my life. I wanted to do nothing but cry and shed grief but you can't do that. Of course, there are days when you get up and you don't want to do a thing and then it takes a real effort to carry on.

It got to the stage that whenever the thought of going to Omagh was mentioned I felt physically ill and there were times when this brought on vomiting, that's how bad it was, so we stopped going down. We just couldn't face it. I was all for the civil action and of bringing these people to justice but the more I learned about it and the more I came to understand it and what was going to happen, the more I thought about it the more I didn't think I could go through it.

You know the saying that people have that time is a great healer, well it's a heap of shit let me tell you. I feel the same today as when it happened. There are days when I get up and it feels so bad and other days when it feels a bit less bad and those are the days you have to hope for, and that's the same for all of us. Your outlook on life changes completely.

I probably don't let the children do what I would have done if we hadn't lost Sean. My daughter is fifteen and it's hard to let her go shopping because of what happened. It's even worse if she wants to go anywhere far away. I hate the student trips now, the summer exchange because it just drives me crazy. I have got a lot of Sean's things still here. Birthdays, Christmas and the anniversary are automatically bad times, but it's the wee things like his

69

mates who are seventeen now and going to discos and I think that should have been my son. It seems like a lifetime since I held him. If somebody had said to me before I lost a child that you will feel exactly the same five years later I wouldn't have believed them. I would have thought maybe a couple of years, that you're going to be broken-hearted but that you would still move on; it's going to have to ease. But it just doesn't.

You get strength from being able to live through it but you're never going to cope with it, or understand it, or come to terms with it. One day you're feeling better, even laughing and carrying on and it might not be a day, it might be a bit longer or it might be just a brief moment. But then you have to deal with the times when you just don't want to get out of bed. It's a strange way to have to live and it's scary that this continues to be how you live after these years. I'm a lot less patient with people as well. If I have something to say I just say it.

Your outlook on life just changes completely, you don't worry about what you used to. You worry about different things. I used to be the world's worst worrier. I would worry about everything. If a bill wasn't paid it would worry me to tears. Now they can line up and it wouldn't bother me. It's clear to me now that life really is too short.

Victor Barker

Victor Barker lost his twelve-year-old son James in the bomb. James was one of the children who was on the day trip with Spanish students to Omagh from Buncrana. Victor and his family have since left Buncrana and Victor works as a solicitor in a town near Guildford in Surrey. I talk with Victor in his office at work. Victor has a photograph of James on his desk.

At the time of his death he was twelve years old and a very, very athletic and fit young guy. He was a great runner, played a lot of football and loved sport. I wouldn't say academically he shone and he was very slightly dyslexic, but he was very easy to get on with and the kids at school really loved him. He was a nice guy, and he was gentle guy. He wasn't at all aggressive. I married my wife Donna twenty years ago and she originally came from Londonderry, or Derry City as she calls it. Donna and I met when she was over in England. We got married and we had a daughter and a son, James. My daughter, Estella, is two years older than James. Much later we had another son called Oliver.

Donna's mother and father had retired to Buncrana, because her mother had come from Derry, they always wanted to go back and it was always my wife's dream to go back again. When her parents retired there, we visited them a couple of times and it is a beautiful country, picturesque, very rugged, mountainous, a beautiful place to live. My wife thought it [would] be a good idea if we bought a house over there and educated the kids there as well. I had my misgivings about it, but she was keen and eventually we made a decision to sell our house in England and buy a house out in Buncrana.

James was at Foyle and Londonderry Prep and got on very well with the other kids. In particular he loved sport and athletics. I would come over every other weekend from England, take a flight over on a Friday night and come back on a Monday morning. He really enjoyed it over there, you know, because it was a different type of life, there was so much more to do in terms of outdoor activities. We lived right by the sea, and he could go walking, rock climbing, play for the football club and take part in local athletics.

One thing people told us about him after he died, is that he would always go up to people and start a conversation. Some kids just don't speak to adults, but he would go straight up to them and say 'I'm James Barker what's your name?' Yes, he would chat to people, and was just a really sunny little guy.

Although he struggled with his reading and writing, he was very bright. He was always very shrewd and kids at school liked him because he could always get hold of things that they wanted. He would know where to get things and he was always liked for that. He got on well with the guys there.

My parents-in-law had Spanish students staying with them, because there was a big link between Buncrana and Madrid. Spanish schools would bring over students and families in Buncrana would look after them. They paid their food and their lodging but the families would look after them.

I came over, that one weekend, because I'd joined a golf club up on the Malin Head and I'd put a team in for the Pro-Am. I'd brought three of my best friends over from England with me on the Thursday night to play two rounds of golf in this competition.

The following morning we got up early to go and play a round of golf, and I asked James if he wanted to come up to the golf course and caddy, but he said that what he would rather go fishing.

So we booked one of the local fishermen for the Friday afternoon and we went all the way up the Lough and down again, and I remember him sitting on my lap and saying 'Dad this is a great place, the only sad thing is that you're not here every day', because obviously I had to work.

You know how some kids when they get to a certain age they pick something up, well with James it was fishing. He wanted to take his rod with him everywhere. That morning we got up very early and I'd gone into the breakfast room and James was there with, with Lucretia, who was the Spanish girl staying with us. About ten minutes later I remember Fernando, another student, coming in through the door and asking if James would be going on a trip to the Folk Park.

Initially I thought Estella was going but she had felt unwell. Fernando stressed that he wanted James to go and I said that if he wanted to he could. So in a real rush

Donna gets into the car with the two boys and off she goes down into town and that's the last I see of the two boys and Lucretia.

Donna says she always remembers him just jumping out of the car because he couldn't wait to get on the bus. They were almost late for the bus when they got down to the town, but there was a minute to go and they made it.

Anyway, we played our round of golf and came back, and we were going out for a meal. We got ready, and Donna rang her Mum up, who is just down the road and said that she was going to be late and asked her Mum if she would pick the kids up and bring them back to the house. We met my friends at the hotel and went down to the St. John's Restaurant and we started our meal, which was about 7 o'clock.

About 7.30pm Donna's mother came in and said that there was no sign of the kids and that there was some problem, an accident of some kind. Of course that immediately petrified Donna and we went to find out what was going on. We said goodbye to the boys and Donna and I drove up to the church.

There was no sign of the kids and nobody was saying anything about an accident so we went to the Garda station. At the station they told us that there was a problem and that all the phone lines to Omagh were down. The man told us about the list of hospitals and recommended we contact them. Nobody knew it was a bomb at the time. So we were ringing the hospital in Londonderry, all the big hospitals in Belfast and elsewhere to try and find out where he was.

We then got a telephone call at about 10 o'clock from one of our neighbours saying there had been something very serious, and it was linked to a bomb. We were advised to sit by the phone and wait for calls. At about this time we discovered that Lucretia, or someone with her name, was actually in a hospital in Belfast. Of course, apart from anything else I felt very responsible to her Mum and Dad, because she was in our care.

I didn't know what to do at that point, whether to go to Belfast or not. The Garda couldn't do anything and couldn't tell us anything, so I said to Donna that I would wait for another hour and if there was no news that I would go to this theme park and find out what had happened.

We waited a bit longer, and about 11.15pm we get a telephone call from Father Shane Bradley, the local priest for Buncrana, who asked me to go to Omagh. I didn't know where it was but we went over the bridge in Derry down through Strabane and after a couple of wrong turns got on the Omagh road. As we get into Omagh there was police roadblocks everywhere. I said that I had come to look for my son and two Spanish students. They told me what had happened and we went down through the town to a Leisure Centre.

I remember going in this place and there was hundreds of people in there. Donna was immediately taken away for a cup of tea. I was asked if I was the father of an English boy and when I said yes was told that I would need to be spoken to. As soon as they started asking me about his hair colour, any distinguishing marks, I knew there was something seriously wrong, and I asked whether he was alive, dead or injured. The guy told me that he didn't know and that enquiries were ongoing.

This went on for hours and hours and hours throughout the night and was just like a waking nightmare. We were in a room, with the priest there from Buncrana along with the Dohertys and the McLaughlins also trying to find out about their children.

We were just kept waiting and waiting; the eternal waiting.

I knew in my heart that there was something very, very seriously wrong. I had never been in this situation before. The priest kept coming in warning us that things looked very bad, but both Donna and I knew that things were very bad anyway.

About 6 o'clock in the morning we get carted off in this car. We were the last to go literally, for whatever reason, to a makeshift mortuary in the Army barracks, and I knew the moment we walked in that was it. Everything was draped in black, there were flowers there and we knew we weren't being brought there to see him in hospital.

After about an hour each one of us was dragged into this little room individually, because there were about seven families there altogether, to identify their child, or their wife. When we identified James, his hair was very, very badly burned and he had a lot of marks and cuts. I remember my wife picking up his hand which was all broken and there was a lot of wailing.

Then we get transported back to the Leisure Centre, and by this stage we had discovered Fernando had died and Lucretia who was very, very badly injured, had been taken to hospital in Belfast. I don't even know how I drove home, because I'd no sleep and I was in a complete state. Of course my wife was hysterical, she couldn't believe what had happened.

I drove home to Buncrana and had to talk to Fernando's Mum because she was in Spain. I had a bit of rest though I didn't sleep, and Donna was there and her parents arrived, and I said that I would have to go to the hotel and tell my friends what had happened.

So I drove down to the hotel and I remember as I got in the foyer of the hotel there was a Sunday newspaper with a picture on the front of James on a stretcher, and it said 'Victim of the Omagh Bomb'. I had just got hold of the paper when my mates came down the stairs and they asked me if James was okay. I said 'Look what they've done to my boy' and I broke down. They tried to help me as much as they could. I explained that I had to go to Belfast to see this poor girl and then we drove down to Belfast with a neighbour. Luckily we picked up the mother at the airport, and she came to the hospital to see the girl, and I felt terrible that this had happened to her daughter who was in our care.

The next day I said to Donna that I had to go back to Omagh to see where James had died. I got in the car and drove all the way back to Omagh and I remember coming across the bridge when this huge RUC guy came up to me and said that the place was out of bounds. I told him that I had come to see where my son had died. After some exchanges they eventually put me in like these boots and allowed me into the site, which was just horrendous. There was blood and bits of clothing everywhere. You could see the hole in the road where the car had exploded, and all the buildings had collapsed. There was rubble and water everywhere, bits of cars and shop windows pummelled in.

I rang the Sunday paper which I had seen the picture in and asked how they could possibly print a picture of my dead son on the cover. Obviously the guy knew I was a bit distraught and apologised. He also said that at the time of the photograph it was not known whether James was dead or not.

Eventually I get a phone call from the guy who had taken the picture, and he came to meet me on the bridge. He got out of his car and was apologetic, but he also insisted that when the photograph was taken James was alive. It turned out that he was still alive and that he hadn't died on the side of the road like some of the others had.

They had found him, they had taken him to the hospital, but he had been left there for an hour and a half bleeding to death, and nobody had had the time to pay any attention to him. Because no one was with him, we weren't there with him, he didn't have his friends, his family, and he was just lying there to all intents and purposes, they didn't know how badly injured he was.

All of a sudden they put him in intensive care and noticed his pressure was going down and apparently they rushed him into the theatre about 6.30pm and he died about 7 o'clock. His spleen had ruptured and the force of the blast had literally knocked him on to a roof and shattered his body internally. That's what killed him, his heart couldn't hold out from the loss of blood, and they were trying work on his spleen.

It was just total indiscrimination. You're there in a town with a thousand people milling about and it's pot luck whether you are one of them. It's affected so many different people in different ways, and I don't begin to try and understand how people feel because each person has to deal with their own grief in the way they feel fit. My wife became very aggressive for a while, very angry. She was totally shocked that this had happened. As a result, she became very depressed. The trauma of going to the wretched mortuary, being dragged off there, and going to collect his body from the Chapel of Rest and bringing him back to Buncrana was unimaginable. Then there's the whole trauma of the funeral which was just literally taken out of our hands.

In retrospect that was my biggest mistake, allowing him to be buried in Buncrana and not taking control at that time. There was Martin McGuiness and Gerry Adams sitting there, and David Trimble and the Ambassador and so on, and I didn't want that for my son, I didn't want a funeral like that, but we were railroaded into it. Later we disinterred him and brought him home to England. We had to get a licence to do it.

The person in my family who it has particularly affected is Estella. She was the closest to James's age and I think she still feels it badly today. She blames herself and believes that it should have been her instead of James. The guilt has had a bad impact.

People were coming to the house, which I found very odd, the coffin was left open and people were coming in, and sprinkling holy water on him and doing this and that. I couldn't handle that at all. You also had all politicians making trite statements and I decided that I didn't want any more to do with it.

What surprised me in the initial months was the vastly disparate reaction from people that I know through business – clients and friends. The majority of them are vastly supportive and would do anything to help. You ask them to go to a fund raising dinner, or you ask them to do something for golf or to raise some money for the Omagh fund and they would do anything. But you get a very small number that don't want to know – violence, terrorism, they don't want anything to do with it – and they all step away.

You always get your low spots, and I think mostly that happens when you do nothing. If you're sitting down at home and you've got nothing on your mind, your thoughts turn. I always remember him and I see him every day when I look at his picture and I see him in my eye hundreds of times and I feel very desperate when I see kids of seventeen who have been out playing golf with their dads. He's not there, and I just think it's desperately unfair for him. I cannot understand these people. How they feel they've got the right to take another human life because of a perceived cause is beyond me.

I no longer fear dying. When you've had a young son die in front of you, it makes the scale of your own life far less significant. You feel guilty about living on when your child is not alive. It's a strange thing to say and I know my wife feels exactly the same but I have faced up to that fact more readily than I would do if my children had all been alive and with me.

I can't tell you whether Omagh is the end of the Troubles, but I would like to think it will be.

Marion Radford

I interview Marion at the Victims Group Office in Omagh. Marion lost her son Alan who was sixteen. Marion shows me a photograph of Alan and talks about him for about an hour.

Alan had a beautiful nature and was a lovely lad that helped me a lot at home. He wasn't like a normal sixteen-year-old you know, playing football and going to discos. He just liked helping, and he particularly liked helping people. He was always helping the neighbours or watching their children for them. He went out too of course, like any sixteen-year-old, but he was wiser for his years.

He was the second youngest of my children. He just had a lovely happy nature. He loved reading and he read about the famine in Ireland. He also loved the film the *Titanic* and went to see that three times. He went with me to see that not long before he died. He was very much an emotional and caring person.

Alan and I always went to town on a Saturday afternoon, because Alan was like my best friend you know, I'm divorced and he went everywhere with me. That's why I miss him so much. Not only did I lose a son that day, but I lost my best friend, the one who I talked my problems out with.

We were supposed to be going to town earlier that day and Alan had said to me the night before that he didn't want to go. I thought that was strange and not like Alan and he sounded a bit down, which wasn't like him at all. But when he got up that morning he said he would go but that we should go later.

Firstly, he went to visit a woman that he used to babysit for, and he was a bit late coming back, that's why we went into town later than normal. We were going to go to shops out of town but then we changed our minds and continued into Omagh.

We were walking because I don't drive, and we got into the town when we saw a girl who knew us. She told us that there might be a bomb but we thought that she must be wrong. I said to Alan it could be true but he thought it was probably a mistake or a hoax.

So we then went into the electrical shop because Alan liked electrical things. I wanted to get money out of the Northern Bank because Alan was going to open a bank account and was planning to do a course. He had just left school and he was going to do a course in catering.

We came out of the electrical shop and we were heading up the road when someone told us that we wouldn't get through because there was a bomb scare. I was looking in a jewellers and Alan wanted to go back across the road.

I walked into the jewellers and I walked back out and I saw the girls closing up the shop and I thought there's something funny going on, I just had this uneasy feeling. As we walked away I suggested to Alan that we go to another part of the town.

At that point he said that he was just going up the road a little way and I went into a shop to get some salad stuff for a meal later. I went into the shop, but I just had this uneasy feeling and it was getting stronger. I thought right, I'm getting Alan and we're getting out of here. I went to pick up some tomatoes and lettuce, was giving the man at the counter the money, when at that split second the bomb went off, and it threw me back.

That's all I know, I can't remember everything from that time because I went into complete shock, I couldn't even scream. For a minute I couldn't remember anything and then I thought about Alan and whether he was okay. I was sure he'd be okay somehow and that God would be looking after him, because I did have great faith in God. But I was really, really scared, and the back of my head was injured because glass from the windows had stuck in my head.

There was a big bit of glass embedded in my head, and when I pulled it out I felt nothing, I was that numb with the shock. I headed out the shop but when I got outside I saw people lying in the rubble. I walked down to the corner, and it was just chaos.

At the beginning when the bomb went off there was just silence and then I heard all these screams. I asked someone that I knew if they had seen Alan, but they hadn't. I was really scared and my only thought was to find him. I didn't know at this time that Alan was lying dead only yards away from me. I don't know how I didn't come across his body then, but I didn't. I started to go up to the electrical shop because that's where he would have been, but this man stopped me and asked me for my coat.

I was acting normal as if nothing had happened, but I was in shock. I gave the man my coat and he covered someone up, I nearly stood on the person and I know now that it was Lorraine Wilson. The man was attending to her. I started to head on up through the town when a girl told me to go to hospital because I was bleeding heavily. I said that I had to find Alan but the girl said that the police had probably found him. I protested about going but by this time the blood was just running down me. I had a white T-shirt on and it was completely dyed red. The girl took my cardigan off and wrapped it round my head to soak the blood up.

She was really in control this girl. She lined people up and sat us down on the pavement so the ambulances could get people off quickly. I don't even know now who that girl is but I really was grateful to her. I said to the ambulance man that I needed to stay to find my son but he said I had to go to hospital. He said they would find Alan.

So I went to the hospital and it was chaos there, the screaming, the blood, the scenes. I can't even remember them that well because I was that much in shock. I can see those scenes but I don't want to remember them, because it was so awful.

With every ambulance that came in I was looking for Alan, but they sent me to another part of the hospital, because they were dealing with the ones that were badly injured or in life threatening condition. After I got seen I just waited for hours to try and find out about Alan.

I phoned home when I was at the hospital and my oldest son Paul he had been out running, so he ran over. I told him that Alan was missing. He said that people were helping and looking in town but that he needed to help in the hospital because they couldn't cope. So Paul went away because he had to help and then they sent me to another part of the hospital.

I kept checking all the lists of people that were coming in, and asking 'Is Alan Radford's name on that?' but nobody knew. Everybody was looking for their own loved ones.

The hospital then sent me home and my daughters got me bathed because the blood was just running off me. The water was red, and my bag was full of glass. Everything I had on had to be destroyed because it was just saturated in blood. And then I started to do some ironing, as if, well everything was normal and Alan would be back shortly. I just had this great hope that he would be alright. But then as the hours went on I just couldn't move. I didn't even go to the Leisure Centre.

Some members of my church went and sat there with some of my family because as the night went on I couldn't move off the chair. I just sat there with the growing thought that he's not coming back and my family gave me some sleeping tablets so I dropped off.

But I woke up and thought I was dreaming, that I actually heard Alan shout for me. I went downstairs but they still hadn't heard anything. As time was going on it became increasingly clear that it would be bad news. Paul's dog stayed with us at that time, Jake, and he was howling. It was like he was crying, and I suppose I knew that Alan was gone, but I tried to resist it.

Later on that morning, about 9 o'clock, I saw Paul and Elaine, my oldest son and daughter, running in and out, and then Elaine told me that Alan was dead. They wanted to identify him before they told me and I couldn't take it in, I just started screaming, and thinking I can't take this, Alan can't be dead. I think I was sitting on the floor and I just started screaming.

A doctor came out and he gave me valium or something to keep me calm because the whole of my inside was shaking at the thought of Alan. Even to this day I can't really believe that he has gone. I was dusting around today before I came out and I picked up a picture (I've got a lot of photos of him) and I looked at it and I thought 'I can't believe what they have done to you son'; just a wee boy in these photos. It's so senseless, such a waste of life, and a life he loved.

His Dad who lives in England didn't come until a day later so he wasn't there to identify him. It's terrible that my son and daughter had to do that. I wish now that I had gone but I just wasn't capable of doing it. I also think if I had seen Alan like that I would be in a mental hospital today.

He was brought home in the early hours of Monday morning. I dreaded the thought of the coffin being here but they say God gives you strength and he must have, because I just felt lifted by a strength beyond my own human strength.

When they opened the coffin up I just looked at him, and it was hard to believe he was dead. Once I touched him and felt his face I could see he was gone. He had a lot of marks on his face, but his whole body was intact. I moved a bit back from the coffin, and there was blood. The undertakers had done their best but they were so busy it wouldn't have been possible to do their normal job, not under those circumstances. There was blood seeping through which upset me but my daughter calmed me down. Although his body was intact, a lot of his organs were destroyed. He looked like an angel, so peaceful looking.

I do believe I will see Alan again. That thought has helped me through. Because the funeral was so public I didn't have time with him on my own and I would have liked a bit more time with him.

Alan's funeral was so sad, but yet there was a good feeling at it, even people remarked how they went away feeling somehow uplifted. But it was terrible after the funeral. That night when we went back after Alan was buried, everybody had gone home and I just felt so depressed.

Not long after I went away to stay with a friend in Enniskillen for about a week and when I came back to the house there was a beautiful smell of flowers because there was flowers everywhere, but there was also such an emptiness. My children are not coping very well really and it's affected their health. They get on with their lives but the family will never be the same.

When I'm at home I'm often very depressed. I'll wake up every morning thinking I'll just be glad when I leave this life and I would say I am a very strong person. I've always got up and got on with things even when I had marriages that broke up.

I don't think anybody grieves the same way. Some can be angry, some can be very quiet about it, some can shoulder their feelings right away and so on. Sometimes I start crying and I cry the whole of the day. But I also feel that nothing can hurt me the same now. I used to be very sensitive and people could hurt me if they said certain things, but I've hardened to things much more since.

I only work part-time because my health is not that great and I get very, very tired when I'm at home. I come home after five hours work some days and I have to lay down. I don't have the energy I once had. I like to do crosswords and I used to be a person that used to work about the house all the time, but I've no interest in it now. I keep it tidy, I clean it, but I don't have the same interest in it.

I said it after Alan died and I'll say it now that I'm glad I'm not the mother of those who murdered because it's bad enough with what I've got to cope with, but if I thought any of my children murdered someone I couldn't cope with that, I couldn't cope with that at all.

Gerald McFarland

I interview Gerald at the Victims Group Office in Omagh. His daughter Samantha was seventeen at the time of the bomb.

Samantha was a person who I would like to be just half as good as. She had a lovely personality and could get to you with a smile. If there was something I was a bit worried about, she would discuss it with me. If I was a bit reluctant because she was going out somewhere she could just change the situation and lighten me up by giving me a wee pat on the back. She was very reassuring and let me know that she knew my concerns. She would say that she knew the potential problems and that she knew how to handle herself, so not to worry. That was the type of person she was, a person who could instill confidence in others. I always noticed she had that ability, I've seen that with her so much over the years and I've seen her friends benefit from that as well. Yes, Samantha had considerable confidence in herself and she had a lovely personality with it.

I don't live in the Omagh locality now. I live about seventeen miles away. As usual on a Saturday I was watching the racing in the afternoon with the plan of going down to town on the Saturday evening, meeting Samantha and going for a drive. She had a 4x4 then and she loved driving it. She was learning to drive and she could manage it so well. She was always looking forward to us meeting and would always make sure that I knew where to be and what time to meet her. The racing was interrupted and a message came up on the screen to say that there had been a serious bomb in Omagh. I dashed to the phone, but I couldn't make contact with Samantha's Mum or the boys, Jonathon and Richard. They're much older than Samantha, who was the youngest of the family, I've three in the family, and I tried desperately to contact them. I rang around and was able to find out that there was a very large bomb in the north of the town and that there had been a lot of injuries and deaths. Samantha was in the Oxfam shop which was were she worked in a voluntary capacity and that was just the sort of person Samantha was. She wanted to help people who were less better off, less fortunate in the world. She had a kind heart.

I dashed down to Omagh and was directed to the hospital. The nightmare then begun and it went on and on. That was a time that you would never want to live through in your life. The information was very hazy and there was just total confusion, complete mayhem. People were dashing everywhere looking for some of their friends, relatives or loved ones. After what seemed like an eternity the information came through that Samantha wasn't at the hospital. It was at that point that along with my wife and sons, I was directed to the Leisure Centre.

We went to the Leisure Centre, and sat there for ages whilst trying to find out what had happened, but it was difficult for the authorities to establish what was going on and who had died. Eventually I was told that she had gone to the morgue in the Army Camp. That was obviously the worst news imaginable. It was the finality of it all. You have to experience it to really understand it. Throughout you are always hoping for the best and clinging onto hopes that injuries may not be too bad. Injuries would be bad enough but at least your loved one is alive. But in this case the news was the worst it could be. By the time we got the news, hours had passed and it was probably 5 maybe 6 o'clock in the morning when we were taken to the morgue. Jonathon came along with me and said that he wanted to identify Samantha with me, which is what happened. It was a terrible moment and undescribable. I can't put it into words.

Samantha had chosen to do that job when she started her summer holidays from her school in Strabane. She was there with Lorraine Wilson who was a couple of years younger than Samantha. They knew each other because they both lived locally and they had both decided to work in the Oxfam shop. Two young girls who went out into the crowd directly to where the bomb was. A terrible disaster and a total nightmare.

We were given all the courtesy and dignity by those people that helped out, such as the Army who took us to the morgue where she was. There would have been others there too, at the Army Camp because they weren't able to accommodate them all in the local morgue. It was extremely difficult, extremely difficult. A very, very traumatic period in your life for a long period afterwards. Just to be able to cope on a day-to-day basis was hard. The best you could hope for was to bumble along and exist. But then the questions started to arise about how it happened and why.

That period was a very heated period for me. You somehow cope with things but everything is so much harder. What was a few hours in my life lasted for several days – people coming and going, relations and family, the wider community and so on. It was also a time that seems a bit cloudy to me. I don't know how others see it, but to me because of the depth of despair you are in, it doesn't allow you to recollect everything. No, it doesn't allow you to do that. In our particular case we didn't want anything to do with the media because none of us felt in a mental state to do it. We wanted to be left alone for a while.

At the funeral the amount of people was incredible. The church was crammed and there were so many people outside, that all you could see was a mass of faces. I cannot recall individuals because of this sea of faces. It certainly had a big effect on me. At that time you get swept along by the momentum of events, so it's very difficult to assess what is going on. But afterwards, as time went on, it became evident that a lot of things went wrong that day and that we hadn't been told the truth about the security situation. It was then that I really dismissed politicians of all kinds, because none wanted to help clarify the situation or help us find out what really happened.

None of the family took counselling. We didn't want it. Most of the other victims seemed to find it didn't help either from what I can gather. But I would say that the family found it better to try and handle this together. That was our way of dealing with it anyway. The sons were greatly shocked for a long time afterward and I know they miss her, their sister a lot. And as you would expect Dorian and myself have suffered very badly with grief because she was our only daughter. Samantha lived with her mother, because we were separated, but we have an amicable relationship and share the family concerns. We discuss the family issues together. My oldest boy, he's in London working in law, and my second boy is in commercial work. But we have always felt that we had a terrific girl in Samantha. She sort of kept everyone together and was just a thoroughly lovely person.

When the support group first set up there were a lot of people who came along and this was because a lot of families were affected. A massive number of people were injured and some very seriously, like the girl who lost her sight. By and large, the injured people have recovered miraculously well with marvellous work done by the medical profession and there has been some wonderful things which people have done to support those affected by the bomb. I would say though, that at least most of those people can try and pick up their lives again and get on with it again. Loss is a different matter altogether and I would imagine that each of the people you have spoken to would say the same thing. Loss always seems to pull you back.

As long as I'm around, I will try and I find out the truth about what happened and I know that many of the others feel the same way. I'm sure they will be telling you the same thing. And it's been a tough old time because your hopes go up one minute and down the next. One minute you think you're starting to find out the truth, only to find out that's not the case. You also have to contend with hearsay or gossip. We've been up against this now for years. I think that for me, as time goes on you are able to cope with the pain better.

It's still there of course and I know it will be always there, the constant mental pain, but I suppose you can get to grips with it a bit more over time. That's what I find anyway. But having said that, there are times when some small detail may trigger off grief. Quite often for me, it is a young girl that would resemble Samantha very much, with her very dark hair.

She loved riding horses and I was just lucky that I had a very good pony for her which I originally bought for the boys, but they didn't seem to have that much of an interest in equestrian sport. Samantha was very interested in it and was very good with the pony. She had a lovely approach to that pony, which she had in everyday life. She got on with people and had a genuine kindness that people were drawn to. She talked about her interest in geography and her interest in other parts of the world. I think if she had been spared, she would have been one that would like to have travelled quite a bit. I would have had every confidence that whatever she might have done, she would have done it well.

Many people might think that the victims are looking for retribution about what happened, but they are confusing that with justice. There are so many unanswered questions about the security arrangements in the town that day and the transportation of the bomb that need to be answered. Somebody has to be accountable to this and it can't be brushed under the carpet. That can't be healthy in society.

We have met so many politicians, government ministers and so on, but all you get is the niceties with no product at the end of it. If it hadn't been for the media, I have no doubt that it would have died away and been swept under the carpet. The media is a very strong weapon and important for the victims seeking justice.

I often think of that short distance from the Leisure Centre to the Army Camp morgue which is only a mile across town but which took an eternity to get to. That will always remain in my memory, that trip and when I went in to identify Samantha. You know Samantha's lovely features weren't damaged, it was the impact of the blast that killed her. Her internal organs like heart and lungs were collapsed by the blast. Some people could not identify their loved ones because they were blown to pieces.

I'm very angry at society about this. I never forget that the majority are good people. But there are sections of society that are not decent and who have covered things up over this atrocity. I ask you, what kind of father would not want to bring those responsible for the murder of his daughter to book? The people who did this may feel that they had a cause, but don't talk to me about it.

Stanley McCombe

Stanley lost his wife Ann (48) in the bomb. We talk openly and at length at the Omagh Victims Group Office.

I met Ann thirty-five years ago, in 1968 and we married in 1973. We had been married for twenty-five years, we had just celebrated our twenty-fifth anniversary the year that Ann was murdered. It was in June of that year.

Ann was a wonderful person, a very, very caring person, and I suppose that's why I fell in love and married her. I think she was the kindest-hearted person that I've ever known and she cared for everybody. Ann was a person who looked after herself and kept herself pretty fit. She didn't have the vices that I have like drinking and smoking. Ann was a very good Christian, and she loved her church. She loved her family and she loved everyone around her.

I wasn't in Omagh that day because I was in Scotland. I belong to a pipe band and I play in a little band just a few miles out of town. On that Saturday my eldest son and I were in Scotland, for the World Pipe Band Championships. We left Omagh on the Thursday morning and I gave Ann a lift to work. She was starting at 9 o'clock and we weren't leaving until about 9.30am so I ran her into work.

When I was away I would phone every night. I called Ann on the Thursday night and at the end of the call I said I would ring again the following night, on the Friday, but she told me not to bother and to leave it until the Saturday night. The last sort of words I spoke with Ann, were on that Thursday night.

On the Saturday we all went to the competition and it was nearly 3.30pm when I registered in the park. There was a lot of folk from the Omagh area over there, a lot of people involved in pipe band circles. Then I met someone who told me that there had been an awful bomb in Omagh. I asked him where it was and he told me that it had happened by the Court House.

I knew Ann was working, but I thought that the Court House would be well away from the shop where she worked and that they would all be evacuated out of the back of the shop anyway. In the normal case of events if things happen, you know like a fire drill, they have to go through the back of the shop into the car park. They would be well protected by the buildings because they're all three- or four-storey buildings in the main street, so if anything did go off, at least they were protected.

I started to think, well, if there's a bomb warning they'll clear the place. We were so well used to it, with bombs going off around the town and other towns nearby. It seemed routine that the workers and everybody nearby would be cleared out. But, then we met somebody else who told us that a lot of people had been killed at the bottom of the town where Market Street is.

We asked the person if they knew who had been killed but there was no information on that and at that stage, nobody could get through. I tried to phone but it was impossible to get through.

After the final, my eldest son Clive and his friend went to a nearby pub to try and get through. The news had filtered around that there was a big bomb in Omagh in Northern Ireland. Then when we got back to the coach there was a man who said to me that he had some bad news for me. I think I went weak. He told me that my sister had been caught up in the bomb. My sister Rosemary was a traffic warden at the time and she was badly injured. The man told me that he thought Rosemary had been killed and I just went to pieces.

We were on the coach and everyone was on mobile phones trying to get through but unable to. We then put on the radio as we drove away from Glasgow down to the airport where we were staying, I was just flicking through channels, and there was five dead, then six dead and then ten. Still, I didn't know anything. Not for one minute did I think that Ann would be down that part of the town.

When we got back to the hotel, the manager gave us two lines in his office and told us to call whoever we needed. I tried contacting my brothers, but there was just no way you could get through. Most people caught in the bomb had been identified but they didn't release names, it was just hearsay and Ann's name was never mentioned.

I remember thinking that irrespective of who had died as a result of the bomb, I would know most of them. It wasn't until some time after 8 o'clock on the Saturday night, that my brother got in contact with me through the bus driver. He told me that Ann was missing and that's when it really hit home for me.

We were still there in Ayr at the hotel on Saturday night and I thought that there was no way Ann would be missing for five hours unless it was serious. She would have contacted somebody in the family and all my brothers and sisters are around the town. This certainly got me thinking the worst. I remember saying to people that Ann was dead and there was no doubt about. I just went to pieces then. Your head goes, I mean, nobody just knows that feeling unless you've been there. Your head's buzzing and you don't know what to do. It must have been about 11 o'clock when Clive got through to my brother again. He found out that my minister had gone to the temporary morgue at the Army Camp and had identified Ann. That's when my worst fears were confirmed.

I tried to get home. I phoned the Strathclyde Police and asked if there was anything they could do for me, get me a helicopter or something. I just had to get home. The hotel manager contacted the ferry people and explained to them what had happened, and they said that they would get us across early. So we stayed on the bus and managed to get a crossing. I got back to Omagh about 10 o'clock on Sunday morning.

That was the worst and longest journey of my life. I can recall every minute of that journey. When [we] arrived home on the Sunday you could feel death in the air. People talk about a feeling of death and you could feel it that morning in Omagh.

We didn't come in past the site because you weren't allowed to drive past it, so we had to come in on a detour. But when we got to the roundabout, which was just about a quarter of a mile from the bomb site, and quarter of a mile from my own house, it was a very strange feeling.

It's hard to explain that feeling, but you could sense it. Everything was so still, you couldn't hear a dog barking, or a car, and there was nobody about. Everybody had just disappeared.

I was taken around to the Leisure Centre where the incident headquarters was, and I had to go to the morgue to identify Ann. She had been identified by the minister, but I had to view her and be sure that it was my wife. I sat there for hours because there was so much happening. It was chaotic with people rushing to and fro trying to find out information.

I had to be escorted by a police officer and I had someone from the Police Authority with me all the time. He was my Liaison Officer and anything I needed, he was there to do it for me, you know. We spent hours waiting to go in and for a number of reasons it didn't happen. So finally I went back home, and it was the Tuesday before I was able to go and identify Ann. Prior to that, I was taken into a room at the temporary morgue, and I was interviewed by an inspector from Belfast. He asked me all these questions and I had to prove to him that this was Ann and I was who I said I was. I had to go through this before they let me see her.

I had to describe Ann from her head to her feet, so that he could match that the description and be sure that this was Ann. That was very hard to take, you know. I sat there and the words that went through my mind, I thought who the fuck are you to question me about my wife. At that particular point I felt like they were accusing me of murdering her. They asked me if my wife was taking any tablets or had any distinguishing marks. Ann had an operation that year, and she had a wee wart on her finger. She also had a crown on her front tooth and was wearing certain jewellery. As I told them all this, they ticked it off. That was really hard and left me very angry.

I saw Ann about 11 o'clock on the Tuesday and that was the longest day that I'll ever live. I will never ever forget it. I see Ann all the time, but that image stays in my head and will be in my head until the day I die. Because my boys were of a young age, I just didn't want them in there. If they had have seen what I saw and the way those murderers left my wife's body they would flip. Anything could happen. They could want revenge because although you can't change anything, it makes you very bitter.

I've never hated anybody in my life, but I hate those people. It changes your whole life because now I don't trust anybody, that's what it's done to me. When I was with Ann, I was easy-going and enjoyed life, but now there is a big void there.

My son will ring me maybe two or three times a day, to see where I am, to let me know what he's doing. He works for a big firm in Omagh. It makes you worried about what might happen to your other loved ones. All I'm looking for here is justice because no matter what else happens, it'll never bring my Ann back. That's part of my life that's gone for good.

People might expect you to pick yourself up and go on but you can't because it's with you every day. When I get up in the morning I have to clean the house, do the washing and do the ironing. If I didn't do it there's nobody that would come in and do it for me. It's a big thing when one minute you have company doing certain things for you and the next minute you are on your own.

There were thousands of people coming by the house. I stood for hours every day and night as people came from all over Northern Ireland. This went on from the Monday to the Thursday. I was smoking one hundred cigarettes a day and not going to bed. All I did was eat to try and gain a bit of comfort. I went from twelve stone to fifteen stone in about six months because I ate, just comfort eating.

I was not sleeping and not going to bed. My head just buzzed all the time. I didn't want to see anybody, and then when I was on my own I wanted to see somebody. But you always wanted that someone who was never going to be there.

There were times when I was in my car on my own and I would drive as fast as I could maybe 110 or 115 mph down a wee road. I wasn't worried and I couldn't have cared less if I had killed myself because it didn't frighten me. That's the way it was. At times I didn't know what I was doing, why I was here, or what the point of anything was.

I had to look after my two boys and keep an eye on them, that's what kept me going. I had to keep them on the straight and narrow and I had to know where they were, who they were with, what time they were going to be home by, and how they were going to get home. My biggest fear was that out of anger my boys would get involved in some kind of organisation.

I think we've been seen as always crying, always begging, but we are not. My sister got compensated because she was badly injured, but she was treated like a piece of meat and a peep show. She went through some degrading things and had to wait and wait and wait. I lost my job and when that occurs you lose all your morals and negative things start to happen. You just can't concentrate the same. It changed me as a person.

I'm not a violent person but if somebody gets the wrong side of me all that's changed. I know there is a lot of people out there who don't like the victims trying to bring those guilty to justice, but there's not a politician in this country fighting for us.

If my house was going to fall in around me now, I would say well it can fall. There's nobody there to kick me up my backside and say you need to do this and do that. You just lose interest in things like that, you know. I always went to church but haven't been in years. There's nobody there to give me a push. Okay, I have met a friend again, someone who suffered a similar fate as I did, and we're good friends, but it will never be the same. It gives you a wee bit of stability in your social life. It also makes it easier to go out because before I hated to see people with their partners, wives, girlfriends or whatever. I felt completely out of it and alone. I get invited to an awful lot of weddings but I hate them. I would rather be on my own.

You know, I never used to swear or curse at things, but now I just swear away. It's anger. The problem is anger ruins your life and those around you and this has happened because of what they did to my wife.

Laurence Rush

Laurence lost his wife Elizabeth who was fifty-seven. I talk with Laurence at his home in Omagh. He shows me his garden and we talk at length over tea.

I was about fourteen when I met Libby and we just hit it off. We went through the usual courtship, although her parents didn't really approve of it because of her age. She gave me a ring which had inscribed on it 'To Laurence on his 15th birthday'. I wore it all my life, and I don't wear jewellery at all, but I just wore that one ring.

Finally the ring had to be realigned again and after she died, about three or four months later, that ring was still in the jewellers. I went down to the jewellers got it and I put it on my finger and the next day I went out and the ring got lost. I never got that ring back. It lasted throughout my marriage until the end and then it just disappeared off my finger and I never saw it again.

We married at eighteen and not long after, landed ourselves in London. I worked for quite a number of years in London and I was very happy there. I got friendly with a gang of Eastenders and we used to go drinking and have a few pints, it was a good craic.

Libby was very quiet and was the complete opposite to me. She was a very serene woman. She was a dressmaker, when dressmakers were highly prized, and she used to make wedding dresses, things like that. I never ever actually heard her criticising anyone, and she always had a good word to say about people. She always looked for the best in them.

She also later ran a coffee shop when we came back home from London. When we came back I had problems getting work so I became a signwriter and calligrapher. I'd studied that at the London College of Art in evening and day classes.

Libby was a very, very talented woman. She started a middle range dress shop. Funny thing is, a lot of the designers, particularly the Irish designers, you know like John Rocha and people like that, we'd known them from when they were in the one room in Dublin. Eventually, I took up a teaching post in Omagh Technical College, in the Art Department. I stayed there for four or five years teaching lettering on Saturdays, Sundays and evenings and gradually I built a business up.

Libby now decided we didn't want a dress shop and started serving coffee in what became Dooley's Coffee shop. Serving coffee wasn't popular then like it is now. We decided to put a few tables in a small part of the shop and it just grew. We had our regulars and there were five or six pensioner couples who used it all the time. I later discovered [after] she died that the prices had hardly gone up in twenty years. That was the kind of person that she was.

I have had a problem with drink and I remember the day I gave it up. I really was beaten and I went out looking for help. I went to a friend and he took me to the hospital.

Libby was so delighted, I remember the first day she came up to the hospital to see me.

I remember seeing her walking towards me with a little bag, and she was smiling. That would have been about 1996-97, about fourteen months before it happened. I was always glad about that, as if it was foreseen. She felt that she had gotten me back and I wasn't going to be dragged out off a bar room stool. The thought of that happening when I finally heard about the horror, that would have been too much to take.

That day I had gone swimming as usual at 9 o'clock in the morning and then I went into the coffee shop afterwards. I went in and was chatting to her and she was smiling. I went across to a fruit and vegetable shop and bought vegetables and stuff for the weekend. I brought Libby a bag of mixed nuts and I remember her saying they would make her fat. We laughed and I said that I would see her later on.

Two weeks before that I'd been to a horticultural show and was interested in buying some chickens. When I left Libby I went to see a guy about getting some. I thought I'd get these chickens and keep them in the garden.

I took off from Libby quite happily and was coming around the outside of the town on the Dublin road when I came across the army stopping people, which wasn't unusual. I went round the diversion and could see across the top of the town and everything seemed fine.

I got home about 5 o'clock and I was chopping some sticks when the door opened and my grandson, who is just eleven came in. He was ashen white and had a cold sweat all over him. He asked me where his granny was and when I said at the shop, he told me that there had been a bomb nearby. I dropped the hatchet, jumped into the car and drove like a madman down to the town, to see what had happened.

The police and the army were stopping people and I didn't even try to stop and explain to them about my fears for Libby. I decided to do a skid turn on the road and go back over the bridge past the Orange Hall and come into town the back way. I screeched to a halt and left the car practically in the middle of the road. I just run out of the car, slammed the door and run up the hill. It was like the fucking killing fields, it was terrible.

I made my way to the hospital and there were people lying all over the place with blood pouring out of them. The place was red with blood and I made my way through, over the legs and arms of these people. I just couldn't believe what I was seeing.

I spotted a nurse that knew me and I told her that I needed to find Libby. The nurse didn't know if she had been checked in or whether she was injured, so I ran to every ward and looked at every face to see if it was her. I went up the stairs to the second floor and I went straight into the operating theatre.

They had three tables going and the doctors were all dressed. I looked at the people in the operating theatre to see if any of them was Libby. No one tried to stop me or anything. I came back out, and I started looking in cupboards, I started looking anywhere and everywhere. Nobody had seen or heard about Libby and somehow that gave me a little hope because I thought she might be in another hospital, or walking around dazed somewhere.

I was told that there were people over at the Leisure Centre and I ran the whole way there. When I went in there was a lot of weeping and crying and people were everywhere.

I waited and waited and waited but still I couldn't find anyone that knew anything about Libby. I spent something like thirty hours in that place with no word.

Eventually, the army phoned me for identification information and asked me if Libby had any distinguishing marks. I said that she had a throat operation and there would be a small scar.

At that point it still wasn't certain about what was going on. I went walking up and down the Leisure Centre trying to comfort people that were obviously distressed. I went to the toilet and there was a big mirror there. I stood in front of the mirror, and thought if I will it hard enough that Libby would come back to me. It didn't work.

I was then asked to go to another room. When I went in they had set out chairs and a table, and there was four or five people sitting at the table. There was a priest and a minister, and they started talking about the disaster, but even here, nobody said anything about Libby. Obviously though these people were there to inform families about their loved ones being dead.

The priest and the minister got up and said a few prayers and said 'for the bereaved'. I stood up immediately and said 'How fucking dare you come down here and tell me my wife's dead. How dare you pray. How dare you say prayers over her body when she's not even here yet.'

Then a young policewoman came up to me and asked to talk. I told her I didn't want to talk with her, but she insisted that I did. I told her that if she had any bad news to tell me and not look towards the children. I just didn't want them to know.

I was then taken out of it by my brother-in-law and my sister, and driven out to their house. My brother-in-law said that we would need to go and identify the body and I just didn't want to do that at all.

I drank a cup of tea, and finally when I finished the cup of tea they seemed to be back again and talking. I said that we should go, but I then found out that they had been. I must have been knocked out, you know. It was probably the shock. I didn't object to it, but I wanted to see Libby because I still didn't believe it.

She was desecrated. The bomb went off not ten feet from her and blew her into the back of the shop. I went out then the next day to the mortuary, but they wouldn't let me see her. The strange thing is that there was a security alert and I was escorted out the back way. Prince Charles was visiting the hospital and there was a security alert in the town.

At that time I went out to the hospital where I met a funeral director that I knew. I asked him to make her look better and he said that he would try, but that the damage to her face was bad.

He did what he could but when I went to collect her, he

told me not to open the coffin. When I asked why not, he said 'I couldn't fix her, I just couldn't fix her.'

She came home in the coffin for two nights and a day. I tried to get people away so I could get the coffin open, but I couldn't. My sons all stayed and thousands of people came to visit the house. At that time I just wasn't coping. I was given sleeping tablets when Libby came home and I shook hands with what seemed like an endless amount of people.

A lot of relatives came from Britain and elsewhere, people from all creeds, classes and parties came and my house was open to all them. We never mentioned politics in this house and there was no need to. Libby loved being Irish and was very accepting of others.

I just didn't know what had happened. I was so grief-stricken it seemed my world had collapsed. Someone had taken a person I loved, who was very dear to me. I had a great feeling of injustice over it all. There was a definite numbness created in me. It was like when you step off a plane somewhere and you don't really think you're there. You actually don't really see things. Nothing is registering with you as it should.

One moment you are sleeping with someone and waking and walking with them, and then suddenly the house is empty and they are gone. The first nights when you go to bed and wake the next morning and there's nobody there, people don't realise what that's like. Libby always got up before me and always played the radio low in case she woke me up. She always whispered my name when waking me. Next thing, she wasn't there to do it.

Gradually this house went to rack and ruin. I was on my own and I didn't take care of myself, the house, or the garden. You are seeing me probably at my best and that has only happened recently. Things were going badly for years.

When I finally realised that I was not going to get Libby back, this emptiness and defeat overwhelmed me. I just couldn't imagine what life was going to be like without her, because although we were chalk and cheese, we just clicked.

She was my soul mate, my mentor, a mother, a father and a brother. She was all those things, and I don't say that without knowing what I'm saying. That's exactly what she was.

I feel very bitter towards those who did this and I've said it openly and publicly. But I also thank all those people who lent their help after the bomb went off. Amongst them were Protestants, Catholics, Republicans, policemen and others.

There are a number of people who have told lies about Omagh and tried to cover things up, but we should also remember the good that people did and how they came from across the board to do it. I thank them for that.

Elizabeth Gibson

Elizabeth Gibson lost her sister Esther (36) in the bomb. We talk at her father's farm in a village near Omagh. Elizabeth shows me photographs of Esther as a baby and one taken a day before the bomb. There are a series of photographs which record her engagement. As one would imagine, the images show happiness and hope.

Esther got engaged on her birthday, which was the 28th July and she was getting married on her fiancé's birthday, which was I think was in May. They'd been going out for two years. That day she was going to Omagh to give flowers to the church, because my mother arranges flowers in the church. She was going down to Omagh to buy flowers. She parked her car in the car park beside Market Street. She had been to the bank machine and we know that because we found a wee receipt, saying that she had taken money out on the 15th. She was going to use that money to get flowers for the church.

I remember being here and one of my brothers coming in and saying that there was a bomb in Omagh. Although it was faint we heard it, because it's only about nine or ten miles from here. We've got land down by Omagh, and he was checking cows. He had looked over in the direction of Omagh and seen the smoke. From then on it was a case of ringing round to see who was missing, how big it was, and what had happened. Soon afterwards, news flashes

113

started coming on with requests for medical staff and asking people who had any medical training to go to the hospitals. At this stage I suppose it was about 5 or 6 o'clock, and everyone in the family was accounted for except Esther.

We phoned all the hospitals but they were in chaos, and didn't know themselves who they had admitted. So we went down to Omagh to see if we could find her for ourselves. My father and my brother Robert found her car, but no Esther. At that stage we knew that she must have been caught up in it. If she had been all right she would have gotten back to the car and got home.

They brought her car home and then it was a case of going down to Omagh Hospital and going through the wards yourself, because the staff had no idea about who had been admitted. I remember me going down and meeting my fiancé in Omagh that evening, and we had a look in the wards but there was no sign of Esther anywhere. At that point the police directed us to go to the Leisure Centre, which was where any information was being sent. They had council staff there and because I worked for the council at the time I was able to use the phone. A girl who was there didn't realise I was looking for Esther. I think she assumed I was there to help.

We sat there waiting from about 7 o'clock until something like 2.30 in the morning. It was about then that we got taken to identify Esther. During that time people were asking you questions about those missing and every now and then there would be lists put up which named those who had been sent to hospitals. Esther's name obviously never appeared on the lists. Eventually, we were taken aside and asked by the police for a really detailed description of Esther, which we gave them. After that we were taken across to the Army Camp, where they had set up a temporary mortuary. I was asked to do the identification because I knew what she was wearing. Esther's fiancé came in with me. When we had confirmed that it was Esther we were then brought back to the Leisure Centre, got into our cars and went home. Mummy and Daddy were there and we came in and told them. At this stage there was maybe a hundred people here. Friends and those who had heard that it was too late for her to be alive.

Because there was only one morgue in Omagh, obviously there were loads of people, and it was basically whether you could get an undertaker to do the work for you, and get a slot in the morgue that enabled you to get your funeral sorted. Esther's funeral wasn't until the following Thursday. In England it's different, if you die today, it could be two weeks by the time you're buried. But over here, if I died today it's two days, so if I died on a Wednesday, I'd be buried on Friday, that's the norm. But, everyone was just so busy, there was double funerals and triple funerals and it's only small round here. Basically, it's one undertaker with one car.

During the wake time, nobody slept. Nobody had ever died in this house before, and a wake was a new thing. It was a scary thing, a very scary thing. The coffin was in Esther's room and my sister, two of my brothers and myself tried to sleep in one room, but with the shock and trauma nobody slept at all.

Thousands of people came to the house. They seem to have started at one house and went round to the other houses. We would have people coming here who had a list of four or five different houses where they'd been before, and would have had another eight or nine to go to before they got home. And this lasted for four days, from about 9.00 in the morning until 12 o'clock at night. It's our religion in this country. A Protestant wake would be from 9.00am until 12.00pm at night, whereas a Catholic wake may go on all through the night. The wake provides a kind of closure, but it also allows for respect to be given. To see the thousands of people coming showed that there was a widespread disgust for what had happened and that people needed to show they wanted no part in it.

The boys were very, very angry and my Daddy who is seventy now cried. It was the first time in my life I've ever seen him crying. My mother has since died. She died on 4th July last year with leukaemia. Up until then she was out riding horses, counting cows and very active. She was diagnosed with it, just a few months after the bomb. I remember me and my eldest brother being at the hospital in Belfast speaking with the consultant and asking him if the bomb had anything to do with our mother's condition. He said that although he couldn't say that medically, stress can be an underlying factor to illness. She kept her health and had never been to hospital in her life. Omagh happens and then she is diagnosed with leukaemia, so that's what it's done to my mother.

On the day of the funeral I don't remember leaving here or anything. No one had slept, and we were all on medication. Doctors were pumping us with whatever it is to keep us calm. The funeral is very vague with me although I do remember hundreds of people being there. Afterwards we were completely exhausted. One of my brothers went to bed and he slept for something like two days, but the funeral day itself is still a blank to me.

We had a Police Liaison Officer to help deal with the media and to help us deal with other arrangements. His name was Austin, and he was an angel. If it wasn't for him, I don't know what we would have done. Being no relation, he was obviously able to keep calm and remain level-headed. He was with us most days from 7 o'clock in the morning until midnight.

I went to counselling once and got so annoyed that I was crying for literally two weeks afterwards. I felt that the once was enough for me. Even doing this, I know I'll be in a state for the next couple of days because it would have brought it all back to me. I think that it's easy to get down and get stuck in a rut where you are constantly depressed. The anger can be overwhelming at times.

There isn't a day goes by when Esther or Mummy isn't mentioned. Often when I go to do something Daddy will say 'God you look like your Mother', or 'God you look like Esther.' They are talked about every day.

It's an awful death and an awful death for anybody to come to terms with. If the police had come to our house that night and said 'We've bad news, Esther has been killed in a car accident', that kind of thing, you may have got your head around it more. But the fact that somebody deliberately went to kill, or to maim and hurt, that's the thing that people can't get their head around. Who would accept such a thing? The people who done this no doubt have children of their own and yet they could blow a girl up who was pregnant (Avril Monaghan). They're really beyond logic such people. How dare someone do that to another human being, never mind my sister. I know a lot of people feel that way as well. I try not to dwell on it too much because I'll stress myself out, and I'll be no use to myself or anyone else in that state. Even after today and talking about this, if anyone raises their voice to me it will probably leave me very weepy. That's how it tends to affect me.

Politicians have tried to keep clear of getting involved in Omagh because there's no mileage in it for them. I have written to the heads of the political parties but have had no response. Sometimes it might briefly come up when the parties are fighting local elections, then they try to score a few points off each other, but nothing constructive comes of it.

Each day is bearable as long as I don't let myself think about it all too much. In the past I have been to monthly meetings and felt annoyed for a day or two afterwards. Sometimes a story in the paper brings it back as well, but until those responsible are charged that's likely to go on. The thing about the meetings is that you see people who you would not choose to be your friends, but who you come to know through circumstance. Nobody would choose to go to such meetings, but people need to share things and see what others feel.

The loss has been very, very difficult to cope with and life is still a struggle, to cope with the stress and grief of it all. My Daddy has lost Esther and he's lost Mummy. Since they've gone when people say to him 'You lost your daughter in the bomb', Daddy would just answer back 'aye, I lost my daughter and I lost my wife'. The bomb accounts for both of them and everyone in this family is a firm believer that the bomb killed my mother as well as my sister.

I'm more mellow now and strangely enough although

you would never expect it, so is Daddy. We all expected the exact opposite but he certainly seems more mellow now than he did before.

We need to know what went wrong and how the bomb got into Omagh. Most definitely there has been a cover-up over all of this. We need to know why and how it happened. Sometimes it seems to point towards a situation where these people were known and their intentions were known but they were not stopped. I ask anyone in our position what would they think and do? I suppose to get these people in prison is some kind of justice, but my sister and mother are still dead and nothing can change that.

Mandy Walker

I interview Mandy at her country home a few miles outside of Omagh. Mandy lost her mother Olive Hawkes (61) in the bomb.

Mum was sixty-one, a farmer's wife and had two children, myself and my brother. Both of us were very active on the farm and at home. We did a lot of the farm work along with my Dad who had a heart attack about fifteen years ago. Since then we became more active with the work at home.

She was always very stylish and took great pride in her appearance. She was very active with the Women's Institute, and was involved in the Omagh Agricultural Show. Mum was very much community spirited and she was Treasurer of our local church as well. She just had so much energy for life.

Mum was in the town as she was every day. It was always a joke between my Dad and me, that if Mum wasn't around the house she was in the town. Mum would always have been in Wattersons (a clothes shop) and that's where she was that day as well. She had her car parked up at the Court House, and when the bomb scare went off she was evacuated so she couldn't get back to her car. She was actually with the staff from Wattersons and three staff from that shop were killed as well. It seems that most people thought that it was a hoax. It was a lovely day and everybody was just standing around chatting.

I suppose the most difficult thing for us was that we never got to see Mum's remains because she was decapitated by the force of the explosion. That was one of the most painful things, we just couldn't get our minds around that at all. The wait for us was incredible at the Leisure Centre. Mummy was the second last to be identified.

There was ourselves and the McCrory family that had to wait the longest at the Leisure Centre. We'd been with the McCrory family because they'd lived beside us at home. I think it was her shoes that enabled Mummy to be identified. I remember my brother went round to the Army Camp and he obviously expected to be looking at her remains but they didn't even show him the remains. It was the shoes that allowed identification to be made. And then of course we had the whole thing of the police coming round to the house taking fingerprints and things to confirm it was her. There was a really huge delay and I think it wasn't until something like the Sunday evening that we found out that she was dead.

I was in Dublin on a day out with a girlfriend and we'd heard on the news when we came back into the hotel that evening. Of course we tried to phone home but we couldn't get through. We got a lift back to Omagh and by that stage I'd been in contact with my brother who said that Mummy was missing and that Daddy was in the Leisure Centre. Daddy went on his own because my brother was convinced Mummy was going to come home. Everybody was just stunned.

The girl that I was with and who was very supportive of me the whole way up from Dublin got into the Leisure Centre and her husband was sitting there. When she asked him what he was doing there it turned out that his sister-in-law had been killed as well. That was the kind of closeness which Omagh created, it touched so many people.

We had the police constantly asking questions about any distinguishing marks on Mum. Obviously there were many people in hospital too that had been unidentified. I remember the lists of names of people that were in hospital and constantly going over and looking [at] them.

There would have been names called out every so often which revealed that such and such had been lucky and was at the Royal Hospital, or the City Hospital. You just kept hoping and hoping but as the hours went on there was less names coming forward. This went on until about 2 or 3 o'clock in the morning and then stopped.

Each family was appointed a Family Liaison Officer who stayed with us through the whole thing, the Leisure Centre and everything else. Alan was introduced to us in the early hours of Sunday morning and he stayed with us throughout. He asked us how we felt about the media approaching, and we said we didn't want the media coming near the house or to speak to us. We couldn't have coped with it and I must admit, we had no problem. Even with Mum's funeral there was total respect with no pushing forward or anything. Some families did have different experiences, certainly, but we had no problems in that regard.

It was afterwards that the media thing really got to us, and I suppose it certainly didn't aid our recovery in coming to terms with Mum's death, because the shock of that was a very private thing.

Being so public, families were also being gripped by how other people were grieving and perhaps that there was an expected way to grieve. I was very angry about the publicity side of things and the inquest was my cut-off point with regard to being involved in the public glare.

There were some key things which still stand out in my mind. Seeing families and during the long wait when you'd been all sitting together there as a large group for hours and hours, looking over at the next table and the people next to you asking for news, desperate for any news.

Then very gradually people being moved into another corridor in the Leisure Centre, where the police would ask more detailed questions. From there the next stage was to be taken over to the morgue; being bussed over to identify remains. We were so desperate to try and find her and we couldn't. We were continually fighting the possibility that she was dead.

I remember one police officer coming up to me who we knew well here from Omagh, and I said to him 'Are we ready to go now?' and he said 'but Mandy, you're not going to be able to identify your Mummy', and I just couldn't understand what he meant, that we couldn't identify her. It was then that I realised we had lost her.

Mummy and Daddy would have been deeply religious, being Methodists, you know, and we had been brought up going to church every Sunday, and I remember all these ministers, who I know were trying to be helpful and supportive, coming and praying with us in the middle of the night. One delivered, I think it was, *The Lord's my Shepherd*, the 23rd Psalm, and I just stopped him and said 'Listen, my mother's not dead, what are you trying to say here?' Even though it was so obvious to everybody else that she was gone, it wasn't to us.

Mummy wasn't brought home and her remains weren't released until the Tuesday. As we got home late on Sunday evening people started coming to the house. We never had a chance to get ourselves together at all, or to even try and make sense of what was happening. There was just hundreds and hundreds of people coming through the house, and I don't know how we got through those first few days.

Daddy just couldn't get his head round the day or that he just wasn't allowed to open her coffin to see her. You had all these horror stories going around and people saying that there was probably nothing of her left at all and that the coffin was empty. Daddy had overheard somebody saying this at the wake and I remember one night after everybody had gone, about 2 or 3 o'clock in the morning, we actually heard him. We were sitting downstairs in the kitchen and we heard him creeping upstairs. He was going to Mum's coffin and he was trying to undo the hinges on the coffin to get it open. He was very angry with me afterwards, for months afterwards, that I didn't let him do that.

There was a senior detective at that time who arrived who had been interrogating some men that had been lifted in South Armagh. He arrived with pictures and they had blanked out where Mummy's head would have been. They had a sticker over the top part of Mummy's body and I remember Daddy trying to peel it off. The detective stopped him then and said "No Percy. You know now that there was a body in the coffin anyway.' That was especially hard.

The Saturday afterwards was the big service in the town. We were told by the local clergy that there was a service for the families in Omagh town centre, and naively I went to that, but I didn't let Daddy go.

I remember we went into the Leisure Centre, which was horrific enough going back into, but you are in a kind of overdrive and you don't think things through properly. I remember we went in and Gerry Adams was in the Leisure Centre and I just couldn't believe it. Anyhow, I controlled myself and we were then brought in a procession up to the Court House.

The Court House doors were opened and everybody was pushed out on the steps, where there were hundreds and hundreds of cameras flashing and thousands of people on the street staring at you. Stupidly I got myself into quite a few situations like that, getting chaperoned into this building and that building. Tony Blair stood and made sure he got his pictures taken with us and immediately left. He didn't speak to anybody. We were really used by politicians from all sides.

I got my emotional support from my family, but it was very difficult. For months and months Daddy would visit the grave and question whether Mummy had been buried at all. It was very hard. I suppose I unintentionally took over Mum's role in the family. Daddy's now calling me Olive instead of Mandy and it doesn't matter how many times you correct him he keeps doing it.

There was a great desire in me to have ownership right from the beginning, because I remember even in the first couple of days that distant cousins had started to make arrangements for the wake and the funeral. I thought to myself I might be traumatised but I'm still here, and my brain is still working. People probably with the best of intentions did try to take over, but it was very important that for us it didn't happen.

Daddy's life was just completely destroyed. Mummy was such a positive person in our lives and we needed to try and keep her positive role in mind, to carry on doing things that it would have been easier to not bother with.

Also, Daddy was tortured at home by all these religious denominations coming to offer him support, because they were pressurising him. Me and my brother had to keep them away and tell them that he's got us and he's got his own minister and that's all he needs.

The inquest couldn't come quick enough for me. I was totally obsessed with finding out what had happened. It was horrific and I still have the files upstairs of all the statements. I also have all the photographs of evidence of the bomb scene and of the bodies too. I can't look at that now. But I still need to have it.

I was able to talk to the policeman who had found Mum's remains who was able to give me the comfort that he had covered up her body immediately after the bomb. That definitely gave me some relief, because I had all these visions of Mummy lying on the street and people trampling over her, maybe water running over her. Mummy was so dignified and I thought she had been ripped of everything, so I did actually get some comfort out of it, knowing that Mum was killed instantaneously, that she would have felt nothing and been aware of nothing.

Whenever I listen to the other victims now and during the inquest, I know that some of them had horrific deaths, or they had been alive for a short time after. I couldn't have coped with thinking Mummy was dying and none of us was with her.

Dad and I will often ask how we ever got through it all, but we did, with each other and with good friends. I never thought it would be possible to see five or six years on during those early stages. If you went up to my Mum and Dad's house you would see that my Mum's clothes are still all in the wardrobe as she left them. So although in some respects yes we've moved on, it's always there with you.

I can tell you this as well, there is absolutely no bitterness in my family at all. Our home is still open to both Catholics and Protestants. Our friends are still Catholic and Protestant. I am glad that hasn't changed in us. Some people are amazed that we allow both Protestants and Catholics into our home, but you can't generalise about people. That's the kind of people that we are, and that's the kind of people we will stay.

Thomas Conway

Thomas Conway lost his brother Gareth in the bomb. Gareth was eighteen. I interview Thomas at his home in Exeter where he works as a lawyer and we talk for a couple of hours. Thomas finds that his job offers him an escape from the past and works long hours.

As a family it broke us up because we were very close, living in a little end of terrace house with three bedrooms. There were four boys in one bedroom and three girls in the other and of course, Mummy and Daddy. But since then, my sister's gone off the rails and I've gone off the rails to an extent as well. I'm living this life of putting everything into my work, up to seventy or eighty hours a week and this is to the detriment of everything else. My wife Margaret and son Ryan are going back to Dublin in a couple of weeks, and we're splitting up. My behaviour is very definitely lined to the 'Troubles' and a lot of my friends are the same. We've got this professional life which we throw everything into, but then your emotional and social life is non-existent. My typical routine is to come home late, drink four cans of beer and then go to bed. I also work Saturday as well and then get into an oblivion before getting up for work on Monday. That's obviously why Margaret's leaving, because she can't live with it anymore. There has been some serious knock-on effects in the family which have been devastating in terms of pulling people apart. This has been especially hard for my parents, who have had to see the horror and its destructive effects on the family.

Losing Gareth activated that, but you've got to remember that growing up in the North does a lot of psychological damage to you as well. It's something you only start to appreciate later in life when you go to a psychiatrist, or when you have developed a drink habit. But, no doubt, Gareth was the spark for it that and blew these things out into the open.

I was in Dublin and I went shopping with a friend of mine and I remember splashing out on a ridiculous shirt. We went and brought some fish and went back to the house because she was cooking a fish pie. And then I switched on the news and there was a realisation that it was Omagh. I sat down and heard the messages coming through about the bomb and the casualties and I was stunned. I started thinking that Mummy and Daddy always go into town at 12 o'clock on a Saturday so they must have been in town when the bomb went off. I tried ringing home and couldn't get through because the lines were engaged. The next thing was when the whole magnitude of the deaths started coming in, from five to ten to twenty and so on. Then another friend of mine who was studying with me at Trinity in Dublin came over and we watched the coverage.

Eventually I got through and it was my auntie who told me that Gareth was missing. I spoke to my father and he told me that Gareth was dead. He didn't know at that point because this was early afternoon, but my Dad was convinced that he was dead. I made calls throughout the evening and he was still missing so then I knew that there was something very wrong. I tried to get some sleep and about 3 o'clock my sister phoned me to say that I had better come home. So my friend came down and collected me and we went straight to Omagh and the Leisure Centre. Mummy and my sisters had been at the Leisure Centre all night when I arrived and were waiting to identify Gareth.

Ironically I had had a fallout with my mother and I hadn't spoken to her for maybe a year. I spoke to her through Gareth because he was in the house, so if I needed to say something I would go through him. I went into the Leisure Centre and the place was just madness. It was always a place of fun, but that day it was chaos with families all around the place crying. There were howls and shrieks coming from all over the place. I went over to my mother who was with my sister and my auntie and Michael Gallagher was there. He was taken away to identify his son and my mother was taken with my sister to identify Gareth. They came back and told us he was dead. We were all very emotional. My auntie told me to go over to my mother and I went over and whilst we were a close family we were never an emotional contact family, but I remember trying to hug her in a clumsy way and she tried to lean into me and again it was awkward. She was crying and that was the first time in my life I had seen my mother cry. It was also the last time I saw her cry. Then we went back to Carrickmore and my father was very upset.

I suppose at that point there was a whole sense of community which took over. Your interviews will have taught you a lot about Irish wakes and funerals and the phenomenal amount of people coming to pay respects. But how solemn and respectful the whole thing was, it was incredible. We went on a cortege which was miles long and took Gareth from the morgue to Carrickmore.

Everyone seemed to be out on the streets, it was a remarkably uplifting thing, the sense of community. This was followed by two nights of wakes and there must have been tens of thousands of people who visited.

Gareth was returned home pretty quickly, I think it was on the Sunday night. I think he was the first person to die. The back of his head was gone and there was polystyrene in the back of his head. An arm and a leg had been blown off and they were stapled into the coffin. His face wasn't too bad, just a couple of marks and in Irish culture that's very important, to have an open coffin so people can be seen. He deteriorated quite badly though and became quite purple in colour and the smell was bad. My sister was using scent and since then I can't go into a flower shop because the smell reminds me so much of the dead body.

Gareth was in town to get a pair of jeans and contact lenses because he had just started going out with a girl. It was his first girlfriend. As far as we know he was in a men's clothes shop and he was in the changing room trying a pair of jeans on when the RUC came in and evacuated the shop. They directed him right towards the bomb car. I think the RUC only realised there was someone in the changing rooms when they were trying to close the shop. I suppose if they hadn't found him he might still be alive. Mummy was going with him but they separated and she said she would meet him at the opticians to get his eyes done, so she was at the bottom of the hill and he was at the top. When it went off she went looking for him and couldn't find him.

When he was brought home I felt the family dealt with it very well. Traditionally a wake is something which takes your mind off what is happening and it worked well in that sense. We had so much support from friends and the community that we were distracted from the magnitude of what had happened. You're also removed from the media because you don't have television going in a house where there's a wake taking place. The funeral was remarkable. The cortege must have been at least three miles long and then once the funeral was over we went back into Carrickmore and we were watching it on television. You're almost dizzy with lack of sleep and seeing yourself on television, it was completely bizarre. There was a joke at the time that funeral television had become a channel because it seemed as though there were funerals on all the time. The ceremony itself brings back bad memories, because I was doing a reading and I broke down so utterly. I was so very upset that I don't like even thinking about it.

The family didn't really talk about it, but became obsessed with small details like finding Gareth's glasses, getting his driver's licence back from the police and watching the other funerals for days afterwards. It was about who was attending what funerals and you got caught up in that kind of nonsense. My Mum's a very private person and we gave a couple of interviews to one paper but they represented us quite badly. We were trying to step back a bit from who did it and the need to get them in jail, and we were saying you need to take a bit of time here and not to get obsessed with going down that road just yet. Because we weren't condemning it, this was construed as something which meant a lot more could be read into it. The paper seemed to imply that because we're Republican people refusing to condemn, so readers should have less sympathy for our family. For days afterwards there was just a constant stream of reporters who were knocking on the door and you just got tired of trying to get rid of them.

My father withdrew completely into himself and became quite angry, but my mother took over the house in a dignified way. My sisters were taken over with the trauma and mourning and it was their way of dealing with it. I suppose it's moments like that when you find out about yourself. But people in the North don't like too much of that. The boys of the family tried to get on with it in a masculine way. There are, of course, various ways of trying to come to terms with loss, but those differences did cause problems at times within the family. I'm almost parallelling my Dad's approach, which is to work all hours, come home and drink. He doesn't watch the television or anything. He comes home from work, sits on a chair in the kitchen and waits to go to bed, gets up, then does it all over again the next day.

Gareth's death was never openly discussed, we're not that sort of family. We're very much keep yourself to yourself and get on with it and I think that has been very, very destructive. We were always a family that liked a laugh and the banter, but now we're very much fragmented. Gareth's death definitely influenced that. One of my sisters has been badly affected and I would say more than the others. We turned down counselling after Gareth's death, but since then some of us have had it. I had it for a year in St. Albans and I've started to have it here in Exeter.

From my view, working and drinking is not just about Gareth, it's to do with living in a violent society. It does bad things to you, and it's not to be underestimated. But I think Gareth's death allowed us to focus our self-destruction a bit more, it gave us a complete reason for it.

Gareth was extremely quiet. He was never perceived to be that bright, he was seen to be a slow learner, but he went on to get eight GCSEs. One of the things that was featured at the time he died was his project for GCSE Art when he made the church, which the funeral took place in, out of pegs. It's still in the family home and it's in a case. It's quite remarkable. He also got an acceptance at Derry University to study engineering. One of the biggest tragedies for me was that Gareth was so quiet and he stayed at home. Whereas we all went our separate ways to Dublin and so on, he had never had the chance to do anything. He had never been on a plane or a train, and he hadn't done that much. He lived and moved within this three mile radius of the house. Going to Omagh was an event. He was a very reserved and polite character.

It was particularly hard for my brother Des because he was still at home with Gareth, sharing the bedroom. I would say because of the closeness there, Des would have missed him the most. Des was very quiet throughout the whole funeral and hardly said a word to anybody. He also remained in that state for a couple of years until he came over to England. At that time he just shut down.

When I went back to work I think I underestimated the significance of the bomb for other people. So many people had followed the story and it had really had an effect. People treated me differently when I went back to work because of Gareth's death. You want people to show their respects but, by and large, I wanted to get on with things and try to move on. Having said that, there's times you think you've moved on but there are times when you know you haven't. Things have happened in my life which have not been good and which have left me in the situation I'm facing, which is mentally and emotionally a pretty poor one. I think I've disintegrated, but it would be less apparent to the rest of the family because I don't live down the road from them.

Remarkably, I think my mother is a better person because of it. I think it shook her out of herself in some ways. She's a more measured and mature person than she was before. It's almost like losing Gareth has put everything else into perspective for her and brought her out of a small town Irish wife mentality. Her attitudes towards things seem more liberal as well. I'm pretty sure that that is attributable to going through such an event. You can hide behind the political view, make that your standpoint and relate everything to that standpoint, but there's no two ways about it, living in a violent society is miserable.

The visits home are few and far between now. I went back for the anniversary but I don't go back much at all. Gareth is not really talked about and if he is, it tends to be done in a morose way. However, I suppose I'm part of that problem as well because I don't want to talk about what happened either. One of my sisters made an album which had a lock of Gareth's hair along with poems, photographs that kind of thing, but that's not the kind of thing that most of us could do. I whisked myself off to London to get away from the day-to-day politics of the North and I think that the drinking has been another escape. To me it's a numbness and I've sought that when I'm not at work because I don't want to think about the past. I don't want to think about what's happened.

Michael Gallagher

Michael lost his son Aiden (21) in the bomb. I talk at length with Michael in the Omagh Victims Group Office.

Aiden was our only son and he was twenty-one. He was never difficult and there comes a point where you give advice to your children and then there comes a point where you ask your children for advice. Well I think we were probably coming near to that with Aiden. He was somebody we could rely on and trust and who lived for cars, that was his whole life. He wasn't interested in football, but he liked a good time and was very popular among his friends. He had lots of friends and he enjoyed going out at the weekend, listening to music, having a few beers and enjoying himself. He was somebody who was never in trouble with the police and he was very clean-cut. Aiden was somebody who was always neat and tidy and somebody who you'd be proud to go somewhere with. It was at that time when everything seemed to be looking up.

We had passed the point where we thought we had put most of the trouble behind us. We had the ceasefire and we'd had some pretty horrific things that happened just around and before that. We had two young men who were friends, a Catholic and a Protestant, and they were having a beer in a bar and a Protestant paramilitary group went in and shot them both dead. It was symbolic of how in a divided society there are those who don't have a problem working and being friends with others. I think there were still signs that things were never going to go back to the dark days of the '70s, where we had on a regular basis terrible shootings and murders, but you know I always worried about Aiden going out in the evenings, when he would go to on a Friday night or a Saturday night. I would always never go to sleep until I heard him coming in and closing the door of his bedroom, which was next to ours. We have two other children, Sharon and Cathy. If I thought that Aiden was going to die, I would have thought that it would be in a car crash or when he was out in the evening. I never imagined that it would happen in broad daylight in our own town in the way it did.

It was a beautiful, beautiful Saturday morning and my wife asked me to take her to the local supermarket. In the supermarket on the floor as we went in, all the daily newspapers were spread out and I just sort of went along and had a glance at the headlines, and there was [a] headline that I will always remember which was "Boy with the Iron Mask Gets Married Today". It was referring to a young boy who was very seriously injured in the Enniskillen bomb. He had something like seventy operations, his face had to be completely rebuilt and that Saturday he was getting married and I remember thinking thank God, at least he was getting his life back together again. We went round the supermarket, done what we had to do and went back home where we both had some breakfast.

Aiden and myself worked together. We had a small garage business, and I done the mechanical part of the work whilst Aiden done the bodywork. We didn't normally work on a Saturday unless there was something urgent, but that Saturday, I had a car which I was preparing for MOT. I took it to the garage which was about two miles from our home and I worked there until about midday when I came back for lunch. When I came back I asked my wife where Aiden was and she told me that he was upstairs changing. He had already been out that morning and paid his material bills, you know, people that had supplied the paint that sort of thing, and he had come back and was changing his clothes before picking up his friend and going down the town. During the time, we were in the kitchen when he came to the door to tell us that he was heading out again. That week his own car had broken down and he asked my wife if he could borrow her car. She told him that it would be no problem. He started to ask about jeans, because normally my wife would have bought the jeans for him, and asked about his waist size and leg size. I told him not to worry about it because they would measure him in the shop anyway.

We had what I would describe as a very pleasant conversation and he said that he wouldn't be long because he wanted to get back and work on his own car. My last memory of Aiden was as he walked down the hall, looked back for the last time and said 'I won't be long.' He then left and I went back to the garage.

I was lying underneath the car, changing one of the brake linings when I heard this almighty explosion and I knew right away that it was a bomb because it was August in the middle of the summer, and it was too loud and too long for thunder. I immediately got up from underneath the car, locked the garage and I went towards Omagh where I could see in the distance a pall of smoke rising. At that time I didn't realise that Aiden was probably breathing his last breath. As I got home I could hear the sirens of the police, the ambulance and the fire brigade. When I got home Cathy, my youngest daughter, was there and my wife, Patsy, and they were quite agitated because they knew that Aiden had gone to the town. Cathy, in fact, had just got back from the town minutes before. We were obviously concerned. There seemed to be helicopters up and an awful lot of noise.

After a short period we put on the TV and the Teletext and it started to say how there was a serious bomb in Omagh town centre, where there was casualties. It then went on to say that there was three or four people dead, then it was five or six, and eventually it went up to ten people.

At that point, I told Cathy that I didn't want it on again because I knew that if ten people had died, then there must have been hundreds injured. I felt very concerned, and I told Patsy I was going to the hospital, which I did. I arrived at the back entrance which is the casualty entrance to the hospital, and I parked the car on the road because I couldn't get that close to the hospital, it was so busy. As I got closer, I could see that people were coming in cars, vans, ambulances and all sorts of vehicles, with different degrees of injury. When I actually got into the hospital grounds, I saw a woman coming with a child. It must have been an infant that wouldn't have been much more than a year old, and this child was wrapped up. I don't even know to this day if that baby was dead or alive and I've met the lady, but I've never mentioned it to her. In the casualty entrance it was completely solid with people, mostly with head wounds. There was a lot of blood and it was everywhere, it was just a truly horrific scene.

In the background on a piece of high ground is where

the helipad is and I could see as one helicopter was taking off there was another one waiting to land. It was like something you would see in Vietnam in the '70s, except it was women and children being taken off. Outside on the ground there were people with hospital blankets wrapped round them. I remember going into the Outpatients Department and I recognised a young girl who I knew and I remember saying 'I'll tell your mother where you are'. I then went into the main hospital and there was a woman on a stretcher. I could tell it was a woman because of the sort of clothing, but she was obviously dead. People were in the treatment rooms and you could have gone into any of them because there was hardly any staff about. I think when the bomb exploded and the people started arriving there was one doctor and two nurses on duty at that time, which was normal on a Saturday evening, and yet you had hundreds of casualties arriving, many of them very seriously injured. Some of the things were quite horrific. I went into as many wards and treatment rooms as I could trying to see if I could recognise the clothing that Aiden would have had on, and I remember coming back out of the hospital saying to myself 'Thank God Aiden's not here' and I went home.

When I went home, the father of Aiden's friend Michael Barratt (who is also called Michael Barratt) had arrived and we went to the hospital again, where it was starting to get a bit more organised, but we couldn't see either Michael or Aiden. Then I remembered before Aiden left that he told me he was buying a pair of jeans, a pair of boots and he was going to the Post Office. I told him where to park the car so I went to check if the car was there. When I went back to that car park there was only two cars in the car park, and one of them was the one that Aiden was driving. And I think for me that was the point that I knew I was in real trouble. I was almost at the point of collapsing when I saw that car, because I knew that if Aiden had have been alive, or capable of it, he would have walked, he would have crawled, and he would have phoned, because that's the type of person he always was. If he was going to be late home he would have told us, and if he had been capable of telling us that the bomb had exploded and he wasn't injured he would have done it. I went back to the house where some family and friends had arrived. I also remember that Cathy lit a candle and put it on the window. I never said that I had seen the car.

We both went back to the hospital for the third time and in one of the wards we found Michael lying in a bed. He was pretty badly burned, his hair was burned and his face and side. He was conscious though and I asked him where Aiden was, but he didn't know. He told me that the last thing he could remember was the both of them walking down the middle of the street. I left Michael with his father and was told to go to the Leisure Centre.

A brother of mine, James, who lives about ten miles from Omagh, was in the part-time Fire Brigade and he was there as a second responder to the bomb. They were called out early on, but he didn't see Aiden on the streets. He came and joined me and we waited through the night.

The different lists of the injured were put up telling the families which hospital the injured were in and, of course, those families left immediately. As the night wore on the crowds got smaller and the lists got less frequent and I remember getting pretty impatient. I went up to one of the policemen there and I said 'We've heard a lot about the injured, surely there must be some news about the dead. There must be some people that can be identified', but the night just went on and on.

I think it was about 5.30 in the morning when I was asked to go into another room and there were two police officers there who were asking pretty detailed questions. You just knew by the nature of the questions, that it wasn't going to be a happy outcome, but I answered them. The process then was that the information would be given to police motorcyclists who went to the temporary mortuary at the Army Camp and if the details you gave them matched up with some of the people that was there, you were taken for formal identification – which is what happened shortly after that.

We got into a minibus and along with other people that I didn't know, but I have since got to know, and we went to the mortuary. When we went in there, this man's wife had died, his daughter had died, and she was pregnant with two unborn children that also died. I remember wondering then if there was any end to this horror. They then started the identification process. There was one older lady they couldn't formally identify and they had to use fingerprinting to do it. We were then told it would be our turn in a room next door. That was a very, very long difficult and painful process, sitting that amount of time in the Leisure Centre. I couldn't eat, I couldn't drink, and I was constantly aware that Patsy and the girls were sitting at home waiting on news. When it finally came, I just couldn't wait. I was there with James, but I couldn't look at Aiden, I just could not look at him. It was James that made the formal identification. He said that his face was very, very black. Actually we had some time to wait on the minibus, and I said 'Look I don't live that far from here, I could even run home from here', I just so desperately didn't want to prolong their agony, and at the same time it was the last thing in the world I wanted to tell them. I think when I did go through that door I didn't really have to say too much. We just all hugged and I said that Aiden would not be coming home.

We had literally thousands of people calling at the house. We have a system of the wake where the body comes from the mortuary home and neighbours and people that you knew from over the years come and pay their respect; show their condolences. That's what happened. I think nearly all, if not all the families in Omagh came, and we had literally thousands of people come on the night before the funeral. In fact, there was that many people who came into our house that we had to open the back door to let them out, they couldn't go out the front door again. The people were queuing for twenty minutes up the road, waiting to get in. During that time, there was one particular spot in the hall where I stood. I just wanted to shake everybody's hand, I wanted to thank them, and at times I was going into a trance but I just wouldn't leave. There were some really fantastic people queuing and it did make a difference. It showed that people cared and they felt it was wrong. That was very important.

On the Sunday, the door rang and on the doorstep was a young girl and a photographer from the *Daily Mirror* in London. As I would normally do, I just brought them in. I think that from that moment I realised this was going to be something very big. I talked to the family about the media interest and we decided that we would talk to them. I think our view was that the world should know the sort of people that died at Omagh, and who best to tell them than the families. I also know that these people are sent here to do a job and that they'll get a story by hook or by crook. If I close the door in their face and they go away and write a story that I don't like, then I bear some responsibility for that. So, as a family, we decided it would be better to try and influence the outcome and have an input into stories whenever possible.

It was difficult, a very painful time in my life, but you know I just felt that people should know the quality of people that died. There was nothing hidden about it, these people didn't even have a stone in their hand, they weren't involved in anything contentious, my son was never involved in any of the trouble. He was never interested in politics, he had no time for it. Our family, the five of us, went and voted for the peace process because we wanted peace. One of the things that was comforting was the number of people from the opposite community to ourselves, who came because they knew that our family was not in any way sectarian. Many of Aiden's friends were Protestant. We didn't discriminate. People were our friends and that was the bottom line. Many of the people that were the first to hold our hand and be there for us were Protestants, and I think it's important that people know that.

The funeral was very difficult. Me and my wife never thought that we would be burying one of our children, we always thought that they would be burying us; the question was which one of us it would be first. It just goes against the very law of nature for you to bury your children, and under the circumstances it was particularly horrific. Father Kevin Mullen, who was our priest, conducted the service and he was very supportive. When we arrived at the church gate and the bishop met us, he told us that he had to attend sixteen other funerals that day and I think that was the first time that I felt the impact of what had happened. Sixteen other funerals in the one day. The church was filled to capacity and the car park was also filled with people. We went in, took our seats and there on the altar was the Presbyterian minister and his wife, and the Church of Ireland minister. Both the Church of Ireland minister and the Presbyterian minister spoke at the service, and I think that was moving. I remember when both of them were finished everybody in the church clapped and to me what they were saying was this is right and this is the way it should be.

After the funeral we were totally and absolutely shattered. Most of us hadn't slept since the Saturday and Aiden was buried on the Wednesday. We just came home had a cup of tea and whatever the time of day it was, every one of us went to bed. I was the last up the stairs that night and before I went to bed I said to Aiden 'If you're here don't ever leave us.' For a few days after that we still had a lot of people calling at the house, but that gradually tapered off, until it was down to immediate family. But it seemed like there was a vacuum and you were in limbo. I think it was at that period that I wanted to know more about the other families that were affected.

After the funerals, then there was a number of us that met up and we started to have ad hoc meetings. Those meetings took place in various locations and that's the way the group started to come together. Then a decision was taken about whether we should try and widen this circle and we held a meeting in a hotel. There wasn't a lot of preparation, it happened quite quickly and at that stage, there was still a lot of people in hospital. But, we had good support and it was then that the Support Group was formed. We went on to meet regularly and it's been a long stormy road.

Then there was the Omagh Fund that was set up to distribute the charity where we felt we wanted to take control in our own lives again. We didn't want people out there talking about us and our lives. We wanted to be part of that, and I think right up to the eve of the anniversary seven years on, we still want to be part of the community. But we feel like the community is treating us like lepers, as if the bomb happened and it's gone away, and we're going to carry on in our own little clique. It's like we are still fighting from the outside to become part of this bigger family. It's as if in some ways they're frightened, as if they don't know how to deal with it.

Then the issues went wider into talks about justice and we got involved with government departments. Early on we had the first formalised meeting and it was aired at the meeting that we were all coming from different backgrounds, with different points of view. It was accepted that when people came to our meetings, we wouldn't ask anybody to leave their religion and their politics outside the door. We would tend to concentrate on things that united us rather than things that divided us, because we knew there were many. The thing that united us was the justice issue, because we had all suffered and that was what we built on. We targeted the Real IRA, because they were the group that took responsibility for the bomb.

Then, I went in 2001, I went to Washington and I spoke to the American administration at that time. That was at the end of President Clinton's term of office and I spoke to the people in the National Security Council, where I was very well received. It was a very moving occasion. I went into the Assistant Director of the National Security Council's office and behind a desk on the wall was a beautiful picture of Tony Blair, Cherie Blair, Hilary Clinton and President Clinton. My eyes focussed on the picture, and behind the picture was a load of rubble, and I thought 'My God, what a beautiful picture, but why did they have to take it where all that rubble was?' It was only then that it came to me that this was the bomb site in Omagh, and I actually broke down. He assured me that the picture wasn't just put up there because he knew I was coming, that it was already there and that this particular individual was very much involved in the peace process. We had a very big fight on our hands to try and get the Real IRA put on the foreign terrorists list, but we did succeed, and I think that will probably be the biggest achievement that we have made because that's the first time an Irish terrorist group was put on the foreign terrorists list.

The Irish Government fought it tooth and nail because they didn't want to have anybody saying that a modern democracy has got a terrorist group based within its borders – you are now being considered in the same league as Afghanistan and Turkey and Libya and Iraq. We have continued to target and put pressure on the governments of both Britain and Ireland.

The peculiar thing about Omagh was that very early on everyone knew who was directly involved. For example, the leader of the Real IRA is known and the Real IRA took responsibility for what happened, so you assume if an atrocity like Omagh was planned, the leader would have to know about it. It went down the chain of command and there were others that were involved in Omagh, but it's a question of putting together enough evidence to bring successful action against these people. And if we're successful, it's not just about Omagh, it means that this is the first time anywhere in the world that families will have taken a terrorist organisation to court in a civil action.

I think if you look at the history of Omagh you wouldn't be looking too long before you discover that contrary to the statements made after the 15th August, there was not the political will to solve this crime, either in London or Dublin. We had the prime minister saying no stone would be left unturned and that all help possible would be given in this investigation to the families. The sad thing is that this didn't materialise in reality.

From early on, I think we realised the value of the media. Next door I've got thousands of newspapers and I'm sure that within the thousands of newspapers there are thousands of articles which directly or indirectly mention Omagh. I think that if we can keep Omagh alive, the better chance we will have of getting to the truth of what happened. It would cost millions of pounds to pay for the publicity that we have got through the media and from very early on, I decided to do anything, to go anywhere, to bend over backwards to facilitate the media. We have a message that we need to get out there which is to make sure that there are no more 'Omaghs'.

We have looked at other major disasters and atrocities, for example, Oklahoma where there was a bomb without warning, yet after Oklahoma there was a full enquiry. A full enquiry not just into how the police, the fire brigade and the ambulance and the hospital services coped, but right down to the churches groups, how the utilities worked, how the telephone and the water services reacted and that report was published. The reason it was published was so that people can see what was done right, where the weaknesses and strengths within the system are, and where things need to improve so that if they have another atrocity or a tragedy they can deal with it better. We don't seem to have that openness and transparency that they have in like America or Australia.

We feel that people have to get it into their brain that once those bombers closed that car door in Omagh that day, it ceased to be a security issue and it became a public safety issue. In the shop that Aiden was in, both he and Michael Barrett were evacuated when the policeman came in and told them to get out because there was a bomb. It was a ladies and gents outfitters and the ladies in the store went along with them and they were all put out onto the main street where the danger was perceived to be. The men in the store went out the rear entrance where there was a car park. The result was Aiden and three of the staff of the shop died. At the shop where the car bomb was parked outside nine customers died and there was nine staff but and not one of them got a scratch because they were evacuated out of the rear of the premises. Surely to God there must be lessons to be learned there? On September 11th, within a year we have seen two reports, not one but two reports, and you can go onto the Internet and see those reports, of how people responded, how it was handled, what has to be done to improve situations in the future. There is a whole air of secrecy here and that's part of the problem.

But, you know, the government should be asking these questions, instead of us. We have got some very practical things that could affect victims, whether it be a plane crash, a rail crash, a ship going down, or a bomb, but the government haven't even asked us all these years on, because they are not interested. They go to the experts, or the so-called experts. Do you know who the experts are? Price Waterhouse, who they will pay hundreds of thousands of pounds to and all they do is go around and ask other people about their views, put it in a dossier and hand it to the government so the government can say well, we spent £200,000 on Price Waterhouse and we've this very good report.

Omagh came in a new atmosphere. It happened in what was supposed to be relative peace time, and I think given the town that it happened in, there has never been the sectarian overtones that you have in Portadown, Belfast and Derry. As a group of people we got together and we said we are not going to let the things that would normally divide us do so. We have risen above that. We're going to hold to account all of those that have answers, whether they be government, police, or terrorists. Although the ultimate responsibility is with the terrorists and we will never deflect any [of] that responsibility, the police, the government and the authorities have responsibilities which they must live up to. They must be held accountable on that score.

Afterword

Although the terrorist act has a definite and conclusive end, the suffering of victims and the experience of loss is a process without end. Here, victims are faced with a myriad of different emotions and attitudes which change with moods, memories and the fluctuations of inner-strength over time. Photographs, family gatherings, conversations, anniversaries, birthdays and the random details of everyday life mean that those who have lost loved ones are constantly reminded of that fact. Such reminders ensure loss remains omnipresent in the lives of those who must endure it. What emerges from the interviews in this book is that suffering in such circumstances is not only about trying to contend with the gaps that loss creates in families, but also dealing with the various emotional crises that can beset families because of that gap. Whether loss manifests into destructive forms of guilt which result in attempted suicide, or whether it pulls a family closer together in a positive way, means that however loss is handled, it is nevertheless at once both enforced and transformative. It is hard to conceive of the changes spoken about in these interviews as being anything other than imposed, even if contending with that imposition allows for certain choices and freedoms to be exercised. The various effects which loss has had on those in this book reflects both the different and similar impact which suffering brings to victims.

The Omagh bomb killed individuals from a variety of denominations and backgrounds: it was this cross-community impact which hindered the prospect of political parties exploiting the tragedy for sectarian or divisive ends. Omagh,

153

in other words, has been avoided by politicians essentially because it cannot be used to help magnify political antagonisms in a conventional way. Ironically, the bomb did not discriminate but politicians have, and this has happened because overwhelmingly, dominant Northern Ireland politics depends on manipulating discriminatory attitudes and positions. Many are angry about the inability of politicians to help in the search for justice, which in the process increases the sense of injustice. This additional frustration merely adds to the suffering of victims who strive to bring to account those responsible.

But perhaps what makes Omagh so hard to comprehend is the number of women and children killed. In the case of children, the bomb created not only mass murder, but the murder of one of the most precious of human qualities, innocence. The murder of this innocence also forcefully brings to the light the defencelessness of victims, their vulnerability and their fragility. The philosopher, Hannah Arendt argues that evil depends on a lack of imagination and a complete lack of consideration for victims, which has resonance in this instance. What the bomb made clear was the complete lack of moral imagination of those who planted it. But although the bombing of Omagh failed to drag Northern Ireland back to the established historical patterns of violence, it nevertheless made sure that the blindness of that act scarred as many as possible within its range. It may have failed to return politics to the dark past, but it succeeded in imposing darkness on the families of those who died (as well as the injured and the psychologically damaged). For those families, only remembering the past is possible. There will be no forgetting here.

The impact of the bomb was both complex and multi-layered. From the focal point of loss, the physical and psychological effects were transmitted throughout the community, from the families, to the emergency services, to the media and beyond. Indeed, the empathy felt by others extended well beyond the immediate locality of Omagh itself. As the interviews all make clear, thousands of people visited the homes of the families to pay their respects and by their very presence demonstrated their resistance to and disgust for the bombers. None of those interviewed sought to advocate violent retaliation against those responsible (an approach which the bombers themselves had no such problem employing) but wished justice to be pursued through the courts, where the legal system should determine the necessary punishment and therefore provide the focus for some kind of closure.

This book could have considered the political repercussions of the bomb but that has not been my intention. Rather I am concerned more with what happens to victims when they close their doors at night and are left with their own emotions and feelings, how they try and deal with loss and how it shapes their everyday living and survival. This is not a common approach to Northern Ireland when the politics of conflict invariably becomes the context for the interpretation of suffering and violence. At the beginning of this book I stated that loss and suffering is a personal process. I also contend that until we engage with the personal consequences of loss we can only remain distanced from it. As long as we are distanced from it, we cannot effectively grapple with the problem of understanding and if we cannot understand, how can we learn?